CUBS PRIDE

CUBS PRIDE

FOR THE LOVE OF ERNIE, FERGIE, AND WRIGLEY

ALAN ROSS

Cumberland House
Nashville, Tennessee

Published by
Cumberland House Publishing, Inc.
431 Harding Industrial Drive
Nashville, TN 37211-3160

Cover design: Gore Studio, Inc., Nashville, Tennessee
Book design: John Mitchell

Library of Congress Cataloging-in-Publication Data

Ross, Alan, 1944–
  Cubs pride : for the love of Ernie, Fergie and Wrigley / Alan Ross.
      p. cm.
  Includes bibliographical references and index.
  ISBN 1-58182-421-1 (pbk. : alk. paper)
  1. Chicago Cubs (Baseball team) I. Title.
  GV875.C6R66 2004
  796.357'64'0977311–dc22

                                    2004022053

Printed in Canada

1 2 3 4 5 6 7—10 09 08 07 06 05 04

For Dennis Flavin,
dearest friend and Cubbie loyalist

and for Caroline,
your courage is a constant source of
inspiration, your love my steady guide

Ernie Banks, "Mr. Cub"

CONTENTS

INTRODUCTION

FOR BASEBALL FANS WHO place a heightened emphasis on tradition and history, it doesn't get any better than the Chicago Cubs.

While sad tales of misfortune, curses, demise, and self-combustion regularly pervade overall Cubbie consciousness, there is only one team in major league baseball history that can boast the timeline of the Chicago Cubs, née Colts, née Remnants, née Orphans, née Colts, née White Stockings.

Cubs Pride takes pride in presenting the story of the National Association's and National League's Chicago franchise, as told by the players themselves, the managers, the coaches, opponents, fans, and members of the media. An all-time Cubs team is also presented, as well as the complete rosters of all the pennant-winning Cubs clubs.

From Cap, The Crab, and Hack—to Ernie, Fergie, and Billy—to Ryne, Sammy, and Kerry—it's all Cubs, radiating timelessly within Wrigley's hallowed walls of ivy.

REMEMBRANCE

THE NINE-YEAR-OLD EXAMINED THE newly opened base-ball card pack, complete with bubble gum, gripped firmly in his small hands. Topps' 1954 edition, card No. 94, stared back at him. Pictured on its front side was a color portrait photo of the Chicago Cubs' brand-new shortstop, coupled with a smaller black-and-white of the player poised in a batting stance. "Ernest Banks" read the machine-printed autographed signature at the bottom. As it turned out, I was holding the future Hall of Famer's first-year card, although rookie cards were still decades away from having their present-day meaning and value among collectors.

That was my introduction to baseball's oldest continuous major league franchise. As a boy raised in southern Connecticut, chances of a migration to distant Wrigley Field were beyond slim. There were no relatives living in Chicago. Fortunately, however, there *was* family in Pittsburgh. Mild initiative found me hopping one of the old, still-operating, electric street trolleys on a Sunday afternoon in the late 1950s for the jaunt from my grandparents' place to downtown Pittsburgh and ancient Forbes Field.

That afternoon, it wasn't the superstar Banks who produced the big day but rather a mostly unsung right fielder named Walt Moryn. Big Moose lined a couple of shots over the right-field wall as the Cubs embraced victory. In what was clearly a case of uncommon clairvoyance and synchronicity, I had managed to wangle autographs from both Moryn and a young substitute backstop named Cal Neeman before the game. I had first heard of Neeman only that morning, when someone from the Pirates organization was quoted in the *Pittsburgh Gazette* with a respectful reference to the new Chicagoan that sparkled with memorable alliteration and internal rhyme: "Fellow name o' Neeman" as events turned out, played no part whatsoever in the game, riding the knotty pine of Forbes's visiting dugout for the full nine.

Years later, as a college freshman, I made the acquaintance of my future college roommate, to whom this book is partially dedicated. He was from Chicago and readily confessed his undying loyalty to the Cubs. I remember feeling sorry for him. There we were, nestled in the shadow of Yankee Stadium, home of the game's perpetual ruling monarchs, while his allegiance was hopelessly fastened to a tradition-laden, losing franchise, then in the throes of the abysmal College of Coaches era that forged a depressing 289–359 won-loss aggregate during our four years in The Bronx. To have stoically connected with this fabled assemblage of lovable—I'm not going to say it—ballplayers who have embodied every plaintive emotion known to mankind is, in the end, nothing short of honorable and persevering valor. Today, I envy him.

— A. R.

CUBS PRIDE

1

CUBS TRADITION

On OPENING DAY OF the 1980 season, a group of fans in the bleachers of Wrigley Field, the Cubs' home playing ground since 1916 [when it was known as Cubs Park], unfurled a banner—on opening day, mind you—that read: WAIT TILL NEXT YEAR!

Barry Gifford
author

The baseball season was almost at an end for 1871 when the Great Chicago Fire destroyed the White Stockings' lakefront ballpark, forcing the team to play its last three games on the road instead of at home as originally scheduled. The White Stockings lost all three contests and slipped from atop the National Association's standings to finish in second place; and thus, the tradition of Chicago teams folding in late season was started.

Larry D. Names
author

Search the records all the way back to the earliest days of professional baseball, and you will see that the Chicago Cubs are older even than the National League.

Jim Langford
author

The Chicago Cubs were born with the National League in 1876 and are the only team to have taken the field in every one of the league's seasons, building a record of continuity that is unparalleled in all of baseball.

Donald Honig
author

In 1876 Ulysses S. Grant was president, Custer met his end at Little Big Horn, the United States had 38 states, and the Chicago Cubs were the White Stockings, for the simple reason that they wore white hose.

**Art Ahrens and
Eddie Gold**
authors

Of all the teams in major league baseball, the Chicago Cubs have the longest history, dating back to 1869. . . . The Cubs have played at more ballparks; had more ballplayers, more managers, more coaches; played more games; scored more runs; won more games; and lost more games than any other club in the history of the game. Simply put, the Chicago Cubs of the National League are the oldest continuously operated baseball organization in history.

Larry D. Names

The team was composed of a lot of half-broken colts, many of whom were newcomers to the league.

Cap Anson
Hall of Fame first baseman (1876–97)/manager (1879–97), on the 1890 White Stockings, soon to be nicknamed the Colts in the pre-Cubs era

Everybody has their own psychological equivalent of the Cubs. It's part of the human condition.

David Fulk

editor/author

In a lot of ways, the Cubs being popular everywhere they go started in 1984, with the team we had, and Harry Caray was doing his thing up in the booth. It's just been going strong ever since.

Ryne Sandberg

second baseman (1982–94, 1996–97)/spring training instructor

I'd rather be a lamppost in Chicago than a big shot in any other city.

William A. Hulbert

founder/first president, Chicago White Stockings-Chicago Cubs (1876–82), National League president (1877–82)

The Cubs Factor is based on the startling statistic that the team with the most ex-Cubbies on its Series roster has lost every World Series since 1945, the last year the Cubs themselves were in the World Series.

Dan Riley

author

At Turner Field [Atlanta] during the postseason last year, it was some sight to see, when the Cubs got ahead in those ball games. It almost sounded like a home game.

Ryne Sandberg

on the Cubs' universal popularity, exhibited during the 2003 National League Division Series

The year was 1908, and if baseball fans anywhere but Chicago were crying "break up the Cubs," it was understandable. In that year, the West Siders [they hadn't moved north to Wrigley Field yet] won their third straight National League championship and their second consecutive World Series—the last the Cubs have won. [In fact, in the 11 seasons beginning with 1903, the team won four NL titles, never finishing lower than third.]

Sheldon Mix
author/essayist

It was '45, and Bert Wilson's greatest summer. Though the likeable microphone maniac is long dead, his chant re-echoes: "I don't care who wins, as long as it's the Cubs!"

David Condon
Chicago Tribune, *May 21, 1972*

Wrigley has that atmosphere. Old-time baseball. Thousands of players have been on that field, great players. There's such a tradition there, even going back to Babe Ruth. You get that feeling when you take the field there.

Ryne Sandberg

The most famous goat in World Series history didn't show until '45. This was a live, genuinely fragrant goat named Sonovia. It's likely because of Sonovia that Wrigley Field hasn't seen a Series since.

David Condon
Chicago Tribune, *May 23, 1972*

Gov. Dwight Green was in Wrigley Field. Mayor Ed Kelly was present, too. Mr. William "Billy Goat" Sianis and his blue-ribbon goat, Sonovia, also appeared. Mr. Sianis presented a pair of box seat tickets and escorted Sonovia to choice pews. The Frain ushers started squawking on those newfangled handy-talkies, and very quickly both goats, Billy and Sonovia, were being rushed exitwise.

David Condon

Chicago Tribune, *May 23, 1972, on the legendary incident before Game 4 of the 1945 World Series*

When the Tigers surged ahead by winning the fourth and fifth games, Billy Goat placed an eternal hex on the Cubs. As an afterthought, he telegraphed owner Philip K. Wrigley: "Who smells now?"

David Condon
Chicago Tribune, *May 23, 1972*

Despite his disrespect for the supernatural powers of goats, Wrigley was rather taken with the notion of a hex. He once actually called a professional Evil Eye, a squirrelly, disreputable little man who was paid $5,000—with an extra $25,000 if the Cubs won the pennant—to sit behind home plate and cast spells over opposing pitchers, none of whom cooperated.

Lonnie Wheeler
author

It was Bill Veeck, in fact, who persuaded the Wrigleys to plant ivy out along the outfield walls, in 1938.

Roger Angell
writer/historian/author

The best-known Cub fixture, of course—almost an honored institution—is defeat . . . and no other franchise has taken so mild a view of its own fortunes as to allow its team to amble along with no manager at all, as the Cubs did from 1961–65, when the day-to-day direction was handled by a rotating board of coaches.

Roger Angell

In 1961 [Philip] Wrigley decided to try an innovative managerial style: rotating managers. There would not, in effect, be a manager, but rather a system of coaches who would rotate from the minor-league teams to the big-league dugout and back again. Wrigley wanted his senior people to have full knowledge of every player in the system and to teach them the organizational way of playing baseball. In a game notorious for its conservatism and allegiance to traditions, the idea seemed positively radical and was derided. But, right or wrong, Wrigley must be given credit for attempting something different.

Donald Honig

For the Chicago fan, the Holy Grail is .500. There are no great expectations here. The goal is mediocrity.

Bill Gleason
former Chicago Sun-Times
columnist

Wrigley Field's most conspicuous tradition is mediocre baseball.

George F. Will
political columnist/baseball historian/author

Baseball is above all a matter of belonging, and belonging to the Cubs takes a lifetime.

Roger Angell

If one had to choose a single square mile that contains the most complete cross-section of the United States, the most fully and fundamentally American place in the world, he could start measuring at home plate, Wrigley Field, Chicago, Illinois.

Lonnie Wheeler

Tradition. Year after year, it goes on. Fans react to us and we react to them. In a small park like this, it keeps building.

Ryne Sandberg

2

CUBBIE
BLUE

No, THESE CUBS ARE not in Cooperstown, but they wore or still wear Cubbie Blue with distinction. For all of us, time begins with our own generation. Like immutable pillars, our heroes stand august against the backdrop of youthful recollection, frozen in indelible memories through the magnitude of childhood awe and wonder. But what a treat it would have been to lay eyes on such noteworthy Cubs as Fred Pfeffer, the brilliant second sacker of the 1880s, or the majors' first claimant to the curveball, Fred Goldsmith. The lore of Wrigleyville pulsates with the efforts of those often overshadowed by their larger-than-life teammates.

Joining the team in 1883 was second baseman Fred Pfeffer, whose fielding skills were considered by 19th-century baseball enthusiasts to be better than those of Eddie Collins and Nap Lajoie when those icons were setting standards around the bag in the early years of the new century. Pfeffer became part of what was to become known as Chicago's "stonewall infield"—Cap Anson, Pfeffer, Ned Williamson, and Tom Burns—who played together until 1889.

Donald Honig

Fred Pfeffer was then the greatest second baseman of them all. All you had to do was to throw anywhere near the bag, and he would get it—high, wide, or on the ground. What a man he was to make a return throw; why, he could lay on his stomach and throw 100 yards then.

Mike "King" Kelly

Hall of Fame catcher (1880–86)

Pfeffer played for the White Stockings during 1883–89, 1891, and 1896–97.

Covering as much ground as a modern tarpaulin, Fred Pfeffer became one of the greatest glovemen of his era—without the aid of a glove.

**Art Ahrens and
Eddie Gold**

Fred Goldsmith put in four full years with the White Stockings, from 1880 to 1883. According to some baseball historians, it was Goldsmith who delivered the first curveball. On August 16, 1870, the then-eighteen-year-old youngster arranged a public demonstration to prove to a largely skeptical audience that, if properly delivered, a ball could indeed be made to curve in midair at the will of the thrower. Setting up three poles in the ground, Goldsmith, working from the then-regulation forty-five feet, threw his arcane pitch over and over again, to the amazed satisfaction of all.

Donald Honig

Hank Borowy wasn't a big guy and he wasn't too strong. We got him from the Yankees in a trade, and they paid $100,000 for him. The key to Hank Borowy was he could beat most clubs. The team he could beat and do an outstanding job against was the Cardinals. That was the team we had to beat. Without Borowy, we wouldn't have won the pennant.

Phil Cavarretta

first baseman/outfielder/manager (1934–53), 1945 National League MVP

Borowy won two games and lost two games in the 1945 World Series for Chicago. It is generally accepted that then-manager Charlie Grimm made a poor decision to start a weary Borowy for the critical Game 7 loss to Detroit.

When it came my day to pitch, I pitched. I had 189 complete games—one in the World Series. I guess I could have made a little more money, but I didn't hold out or do this or that. They treated me nice.

Claude Passeau
pitcher (1939–47)

I'll tell you one thing about Passeau. When it was his day to pitch, he was a nice fellow until he got to that white line, and when he crossed that line, he was the meanest fellow I ever knowed.

Clyde McCullough
catcher (1940–43, 1946–48, 1953–56)

From what I've seen of you, the way you hustle and the way you give it your best—don't change.

Lou Gehrig
to young Phil Cavarretta
during the 1938 World Series

Baseball quizzes often ask who played third base in the legendary Tinker-Evers-Chance infield. Answer: an underrated veteran named Harry Steinfeldt, acquired from Cincinnati in time for the 1906 season.

Sheldon Mix

He was like Wade Boggs. He hit from foul line to foul line, a line-drive type of hitter.

Len Merullo
*infielder (1941–47),
on four-time NL All-Star third
baseman Stan Hack*

Stan really was never given the credit he deserves. He could field bunts as well as anybody, and he was a good hitter. I can't understand why he isn't in the Hall of Fame.

Phil Cavarretta
on Stan Hack

Hank Sauer

I wouldn't trade one Sauer for three Sniders.

Frankie Frisch
manager (1949–51),
on two-time National League
All-Star outfielder Hank Sauer

Before Henry Aaron claimed it, the nickname "Hammerin' Hank" belonged to Hank Sauer, the Cubs' slugging outfielder from 1949 to 1955. Soon Hammerin' Hank would pick up another nickname: "Mayor of Wrigley Field." A favorite of Chicago fans, Sauer averaged better than 30 homers a season in his first six years as a Cub, including a career-high 41 in '54. When the pipe-smoking Sauer would return to his fielder's post after each round-tripper, Wrigley Field bleacher fans would strew the outfield with packets of tobacco.

Pete Cava
author

Swish Nicholson, downgraded by some as a Wartime Player, ranks among the Cubs' all-time leaders in a half-dozen offensive categories. He lost the 1944 NL MVP award to St. Louis Cardinals shortstop Marty Marion by a single vote.

Pete Cava

on four-time NL All-Star right fielder Bill Nicholson (1939–48)

Chuck Connors was a hell of an athlete. A big-time basketball player in the NBA [Rochester Royals, Boston Celtics]. When he came up to the major leagues, he couldn't buy a hit. They jammed him on his fists. One day during a game, I'm in the outfield and he's on his knees looking up at the sky. He says, "God, I gave you $5 in the collection. Please God, let me get a base hit."

Eddie Miksis

infielder (1951–56)

Charlie Grimm was great. He was great for the ballplayers, great for the fans, and great for the Cubs. . . . I think he was a good manager. He knew what he was doing. He was ahead of the play all the time. Even though when you say Charlie Grimm you think of a comedian and you think of someone who was perhaps lacking the ability to bear down or be tough on the ballplayers, but Charlie could. He loved to win. That's all you have to do.

Lou Boudreau

manager (1960) and longtime Cubs broadcaster

He had great tools in the field, the best I've ever seen with Ryne Sandberg. He was graceful, talented, humble—it was clear from the very first he would make it immediately.

Ron Santo

third baseman (1960–73), on Kenny Hubbs

NATIONAL BASEBALL HALL OF FAME LIBRARY, COOPERSTOWN, N.Y.

Ron Santo

When I took over the club, I looked upon Ron Santo as one of my greatest assets. He was the best-fielding third baseman in the National League, and he knocked in his 100 to 110 runs a year.

Leo Durocher
manager (1966–72)

Just as the Fifties was a bad decade for rock 'n' roll singers traveling in private airplanes—Buddy Holly, Ritchie Valens, the Big Bopper—so was the Sixties a bad one for professional athletes in private planes—Rocky Marciano, Tony Lema, Rafael Osuna. Kenny Hubbs was an extremely promising young second baseman with the Chicago Cubs, .287 batting average in 1964, Rookie of the Year at 22. He was killed in the crash of a private plane over Provo, Utah, on February 23, 1965.

Brendan C. Boyd and Fred C. Harris
authors

Objectively, how can it be dismissed that [Bruce] Sutter had a hand in nearly half of the team's wins back when saves were often two- or three-inning achievements? That his ERA was 1.35? That the league hit .183 against him? That he struck out 11 batters per nine innings while walking less than two? He was the most dominant pitcher in baseball, one of the most dominant in history.

Doug Myers

author,
on Sutter's 1977 season (not to be confused with his '79 Cy Young Award year)

The one man in the lineup to have an outstanding season was Bill Buckner, who that year split his time between first base and the outfield. Bill's .324 batting average was good enough to lead the league in 1980, giving the team its sixth batting champion since 1901.

Donald Honig

Buckner (1977–84) averaged .308 in seven full seasons with Chicago.

One joy I had was going upstairs and telling Dallas [Green, Cubs GM] I didn't think Lee Smith was a starter. So, we used him as a set-up man early to get his feet on the ground, and now he's got more saves than anybody in the history of this game.

Lee Elia
manager (1982–83)

Elia was the 15th former Cub player to manage the Cubs.

I wasn't a media-type guy. I wasn't outspoken or flashy. I didn't show up the hitters or anything like that. I just did my job.

Lee Smith
pitcher (1980–87)

I loved Leo. I loved him. But we clashed. Off the field, I love people. On the field, I'm a different guy. And that's the way Durocher was. Durocher was a great guy off the field. He was a lot of fun. He was a players' manager. On the field, he was a prick. He was tough. And he hurt you any way he could.

Ron Santo

Rick Sutcliffe was only the fourth pitcher ever to win 20 games in one season while pitching in both leagues [1984]. Fittingly, the last to do it was another man who helped the Cubs to a first-place finish, Hank Borowy in 1945.

Donald Honig

Rick Sutcliffe

[Ken] Holtzman might have been base-ball's second-best Jewish left-hander.

Carrie Muskat

sports journalist/author

There was some criticism of the trade in Chicago, particularly toward the disposal of Rafael Palmeiro, a .307 hitter in 1988. [Manager Jim] Frey took the heat and stood firm.

Donald Honig

*on the infamous trade of future
Hall of Famer Palmeiro, who
went on to hit more than 500
career home runs, and pitcher
Jamie Moyer, still pitching in the
majors through the 2004 season,
to the Texas Rangers for south-
paws Mitch Williams, Paul
Kilgius, and four other players,
in the off-season preceding the
1989 campaign*

If Zim had hair, it would've been red like mine. He's like a father to me. We're both opinionated. What made us so close was our desire to win. . . . Managers aren't supposed to win games; they're not supposed to *lose* games for you. He won 25 games for us in '89, just the stuff he did.

Rick Sutcliffe
pitcher (1984–91),
on former manager Don Zimmer

Me and Zim got along really well. He knew what my capabilities were. He was really the first manager who let me go out there and do what I did. He knew I was going to get in trouble. He was the first one who gave me enough rope to hang myself with.

Mitch "Wild Thing" Williams
pitcher (1989–90)

The Wild Thing didn't bother me. I've been called a lot worse. There's all kind of things they could've called me. I just didn't want people confusing the nickname with who I was. Off the field, I don't consider myself wild in any way.

Mitch Williams

If everyone were like him, I wouldn't play. I'd find a safer way to make a living.

Andy Van Slyke

13-year major leaguer,
on Mitch Williams

Ah, Andre Dawson. What can you say about a guy like that? A perfect guy. He's everything.

Yosh Kawano

longtime Cubs equipment
manager

When Nomar Garciaparra reached 200 hits in 1997, he became only the 17th rookie to do so. Hall of Fame second baseman Billy Herman was one of the handful, with 206 hits in 1932. Not bad, considering that in his first game in the majors late in 1931, he was plunked in the head with a pitch and carried off the field.

Doug Myers

Quick now, what big-league player had the most hits during the 1990s? It wasn't Tony Gwynn, Wade Boggs, or Cal Ripken Jr. —but Mark Grace. The Cubs' All-Star first baseman recorded 1,754 hits from 1990 through 1999.

Pete Cava

This kid is electric. He overpowered us. He threw everything with velocity, with tilt, with sharpness. They threw us a beating, basically.

Clint Hurdle

Colorado Rockies manager, on Cubs second-year ace Carlos Zambrano, after the young pitcher stymied the Rockies, 11–0, retiring the first 14 batters he faced and winding up with a two-hitter, May 7, 2004

When I was growing up in Texas, I'd pretend to be a hitter before I'd be a pitcher. I was McGwire, Canseco, those guys. When I was on the mound, I started by trying to emulate Nolan Ryan's mechanics and just went from there. I tried to have a little intimidation factor if possible.

Kerry Wood
pitcher (1998, 2000–)

Sammy Sosa's amazing season over-shadowed possibly the most significant happening of the 1998 season: the emergence of Kerry Wood as the most overpowering strikeout pitcher in the team's history.

Doug Myers

I like strikeouts.

Kerry Wood

I'm a Cub. This is all I know.
Mark Grace

3

CUBS CHARACTER

WHAT I ALWAYS THOUGHT of when I walked out of this ballpark when I was playing was that one day I might have to ask this little boy or girl for a job. I always thought of that. I don't know why. My children would say, "Dad, we got to go." And I'd be signing autographs, looking at faces. I thought, *Gosh, I might ask you for a job someday or you might have to save my life.* I always thought of that. I can't explain it. I always had empathy for people who came to Wrigley Field.

Ernie Banks

Round up the strongest men who can hit a baseball the farthest the most often, put yourself on first base, and win.

Cap Anson

on managing

There really is a kind of moral and spiritual nobility to being a Cub fan. It's a way of saying to the world, "Hey, you arrogant so-and-so's, you can keep us out of the winner's circle, you can be snide and sarcastic, and you can make your tired jokes about us. But you can't stop us from having fun!"

David Fulk

Leadership is more or less God-given. The true athlete, whether he has better stats than anybody else on the team, will make other players play better.

Gary Matthews

outfielder (1984–87)

Wrigley Field was the very first ballpark I walked into as a big leaguer, and I'll never forget it. I walked into the gate right there by the right-field bullpen. . . . From the time I got onto the field and walked all the way into the left-field corner where the entrance to the Cubs clubhouse was, I was crying like a baby. It was the most excited I'd ever been as an athlete. It was magic. And it stayed that way, even in the years when we didn't do well. I still had great pride to wear that uniform, and it was a wonderful place to play. I think everybody should have the pleasure of playing in that ballpark for that city, for that organization, for one year in their career.

Mike Krukow
pitcher (1976–81)

There's a lot of character and sentimentality in what the Cubs are. They've always seemed older than the White Sox in this town—I don't know why. They have this kind of *humor* about them. The Cubs are outside the realm.

Roger Angell

I used to do things to entertain the kids and the ladies. It's like what Sammy Sosa is doing now. You want to make the fans happy, you do different things, clown around. . . . I used to juggle balls in the outfield between innings. I played the violin one time for Jack Brickhouse. I'd never played the violin before. . . . That's when baseball used to be baseball, back when baseball was fun. Nobody has fun anymore.

Jose Cardenal
outfielder (1972–77)

For me, every day is a holiday.

Sammy Sosa

I don't ever remember missing but one start. I slid into second base and under the shortstop's knee and cracked a rib. I missed one turn. When it was my turn to work, I went to work and no foolishness.

Claude Passeau

You get an adrenaline rush when guys try to run on you. It's not just about hitting home runs to win the game. You can get a clutch hit late in the game, you can throw a guy out, so have pride in all aspects of the game and try not to be a player that shines in one particular area.

Andre Dawson
*outfielder (1987–92), 1987
National League MVP*

Billy Williams, when he first came up, he really wanted to quit. He got disillusioned, and Buck O'Neil and I went to see him at Northwestern Hospital. Buck was doing most of the talking. He said, "Hey, Billy, you missed a great game today," and Billy came back and got inspired and went out and won Rookie of the Year that year. It's all about that. About having someone to light your fire, to get you moving, to let you know you have a lot more to give, a lot more to do. It's tied into hard work, it's tied into discipline, it's tied into attitude.

Ernie Banks

I always think hit. If someone gets me out 100 times, they've got to work twice as hard to get me out that 101st time.

Bill Madlock

third baseman (1974–76)

I always believed in myself as a hitter. I was never satisfied. I talked to Pete Rose and some other hitters, and they were never satisfied. . . . Hell, if I got one, I wanted two. If I got two, I wanted three. All the good hitters are like that. They're never satisfied.

Bill Madlock

Ryno and Andre [Dawson], the way they played the game, I played the game. Play hard and don't disrespect the umpire.

Shawon Dunston

shortstop (1985–95, 1997)

Andre Dawson kept having knee surgeries, and he never complained. One day he dove for a ball and I panicked. I said, "Please, Andre, don't dive." He said, "You've got to play the game right. You don't want me to play, take me out." I took that to heart. He never complained. He respected the game.

Shawon Dunston

I always said I play the game one way, and that's all out. And if I can't play all out when I'm out there, I'd rather someone else was out there.

Andre Dawson

When I go across those white lines, nobody is my friend.

Ron Santo

Well, Mr. Rickey, I predicted we'd win that flag right here in St. Louis, but now that I'm gone, we'll win it in Chicago.

Dizzy Dean
Hall of Fame pitcher (1938–41), upon being traded from St. Louis to Chicago

Because I've played a long time and I've played at a quality level, there's that respect out there, and that's all you can ask for as a player: Have your opponents' respect and have your teammates' respect.

Mark Grace

There are always going to be people who criticize you. That's the way life is. When people criticize me, I like it. That motivates me. That pushes me. That gives me more energy to do my job much better.

Sammy Sosa
outfielder (1992–), 1998 NL MVP

There was never a ball club that loved a fight any better than the Cubs of Tinker and Evers and Chance. The Cubs of that day relished a fight so much that when they weren't fighting the enemy, they were fighting one another. The story that Tinker and Evers didn't speak to each other for a couple of years is well known. . . . However, the players were bound to each other by an intense loyalty to Husk—which was a name they had for Chance—and by their love for baseball. They were a hard-bitten crew.

Grantland Rice

legendary sports journalist

Everywhere I go, there's somebody that has touched my life and I have touched their lives. They were 10 years old, sitting out there in those bleachers. Now they're in their 50s, and they start talking to me about the experiences they had at Wrigley Field and the joy they had in watching me play. I don't remember all of it, but they do. It really is a good feeling to know that you touched people's lives that you don't even know you're touching and how important it is. Some of them are doctors, lawyers, CIA agents, FBI agents, some are presidents of companies.

Ernie Banks

Nobody will outhustle us.

Frankie Frisch

4

CUBS HUMOR

ONE YEAR, I LED the National League in errors. They named a vitamin after me—One-A-Day.

Roy Smalley Sr.
shortstop (1948–53)

This is one day of my life I'll never forget. It's a wonderful feeling to be an immortal.

Gabby Hartnett
catcher (1922–40),
at his Hall of Fame induction
in 1955

The career of Toby Atwell as player was secondary to the career of Toby Atwell as baseball card. Any serious collector of baseball cards in 1952 remembers Atwell's as one of the most difficult to acquire to complete your set.

Brendan C. Boyd and
Fred C. Harris

Playing for the Cubs was like doing 10 to 20 at Folsom; a fine season for them was one in which they flirted with mediocrity.

Mark Kram
sportswriter/author

We're still about two Cadillacs apart.

Ken Holtzman
*pitcher (1965–71, 1978–79),
on negotiating his 1968 contract*

You don't put a plumber in charge of an airline.

Don Johnson
*second baseman (1943–48),
on Philip K. Wrigley, Cubs owner,
who also owned (and some say
favored over his baseball team)
the Wrigley chewing gum company*

I don't think neither one of us was as slow as everyone thought. When you hit home runs, you don't have to be fast.

Ralph Kiner
*outfielder (1953–54),
on the generally accepted belief
that he and fellow Cubs outfielder
Hank Sauer were slow afoot*

Catching the final out of the [1998] wild card game? Better than sex.

Mark Grace

Sex is great, and playing the trumpet is out of sight, but there is no greater thrill than hitting a baseball.

Carmen Fanzone
infielder-outfielder (1971–74)

Fanzone, who later played trumpet in the Tonight Show *band, hit pinch-hit home runs in consecutive at-bats in 1974.*

He used to quote "Casey at the Bat" on the bus. Tucson to Mesa, Mesa to Tucson. It got be where he should've been an actor before he was a ballplayer. We'd go into a restaurant, four of us together, and if there was an empty mike on the stage, he'd turn around and start quoting "Casey at the Bat." He was tremendous. He was a good actor.

Eddie Miksis
on first baseman-turned-Hollywood actor Chuck (The Rifleman) Connors (1951)

This is definitely not an eighth-place club.

Leo Durocher

referring to the Cubs' 1965 finish. He was right. They were a 10th-place team, as events turned out at the conclusion of his first year at the helm

The Cubs are quiche and white wine. The Sox are Polish sausage and draft beer. The Cubs are fern bars. The Sox are neighborhood taverns. The Cubs are power lunches. The Sox are heavy lunch pails. The Cubs are Ralph Lauren. The Sox are Oscar de la Rumpled. Cub fans are sopranos. Sox fans are basses.

Phil Hersh

sports journalist

If a man tells you he's a fan of both the Sox and the Cubs, check your wallet, make sure your watch is still on your wrist, and lock your car doors. It doesn't work out that way in Chicago.

Jay Johnstone
outfielder (1982–84)/author

When I was a kid, I used to pray that the Cubs and White Sox would merge. It would settle all the differences, and then Chicago would have only one bad team.

Tom Dreesen
comedian/Cubs fan

The 1947 to 1967 Cubs years were leaner than Cher. They never won a game they should have lost in that span.

Rick Schwab
author

The Cubs and Phillies staged a comic opera arranged to the tune of base hits.

Frank Schreiber

Chicago Tribune *sportswriter, on the 26–23 slugfest at Wrigley Field, won by the Cubs on August 26, 1926, that featured 51 hits by both clubs—26 by Philadelphia, 25 by Chicago*

This proves the NL doesn't need the DH.

Danny Ozark

Phillies manager (1973–79), on the combined 50 hits recorded by the Phillies and the Cubs during Philadelphia's 23–22 victory over Chicago, May 1, 1979—53 years after the Cubs and Phillies combined for 49 runs in a game

There's nothing wrong with this team that more pitching, more fielding, and more hitting couldn't help.

Bill Buckner

I can give up home runs anywhere.

Dennis Eckersley
*pitcher (1984–86),
on giving up gopher balls at both
Wrigley Field and Fenway Park,
where he pitched for eight years*

Eckersley was inducted into the Hall of Fame in 2004.

The Cubs have been playing without players for years. Now they're going to try it without a manager.

Anonymous
*on the "College of Coaches"
fiasco, in which the Cubs rotated
a body of managers during the
1961 and '62 seasons*

When Leo [Durocher] touched his nose, it meant the hit-and-run was on. But there was a problem: He was always picking his nose.

Herman Franks
manager (1977–79), coach (1970)

In 1891, 40-year-old Cap Anson was hitting under .300 for the first time in his career, and writers began hinting he should retire. So, on September 4, he played an entire game wearing false whiskers in mockery of his detractors.

**Art Ahrens and
Eddie Gold**

I had one this season. . . . I must have gone to the plate at least six times without getting a hit.

Rogers Hornsby
*second baseman/manager
(1929–32) and Hall of Famer,
on batting slumps*

I'd rather hit home runs. You don't have to run as hard.

> **Dave Kingman**
> *outfielder (1978–80),*
> *who had three three-homer games*
> *as a Cub (second in club annals)*

When the pitch is so fat
That the ball hits the bat,
That's Zamora.

> **Anonymous**
> *on closer Oscar Zamora (1974–76)*

I pitch like my hair is on fire.

> **Mitch Williams**

I was watching a spider crawl through the ivy. What else was there to do out there in a game like this?

> **Jose Cardenal**
> *enduring a 22–0 whitewashing by*
> *the Pittsburgh Pirates, September*
> *16, 1975, the most lopsided*
> *shutout of the Cubs during the*
> *20th century*

One thing about the Chicago Bears. When their season starts, it sure takes the heat off us Cubs.

Bill Madlock

Like in the days of the old Boston Braves, who had "Spahn, Sain, and pray for rain," the Cubs have a rotation of Ferguson Jenkins, Steve Trout, and figure it out.

Robert Markus
Chicago Tribune, *1983*

The Cubs are into their 36th rebuilding year.

Joe Goddard
Chicago sports journalist/ columnist, 1981

So the Cubs have not won a pennant in nearly forty years. Look at it this way: In terms of eternity, that's not even a flyspeck.

Jack Brickhouse
longtime Cubs broadcaster, 1984

Any company that invests in the Chicago Cubs has a view of the future we cannot even begin to comprehend.

Jeff MacNelly
Chicago Tribune *cartoonist,
on the Tribune Company's purchase of the team in 1981*

Leo Durocher claimed Sauer's prominent proboscis resembled an automobile hood ornament. Every time Sauer stepped to the plate against one of Durocher's teams, Leo would yell, "Hey, Pontiac!"

Pete Cava

He was built along the lines of a beer keg and not unfamiliar with its contents.

Shirley Povich
*sports journalist,
on Hall of Famer Hack Wilson*

I've never played drunk. Hung-over, yes, but never drunk.

Hack Wilson
center fielder (1926–31)

5

CUBS LEGENDS

Billy HAD A SAYING, "When fish open their mouths, they get caught." Billy didn't talk much. Billy just played.

Ernie Banks
on Billy Williams

In 1878 Albert Spalding retired from active ball. He was only 26. His retirement was a shock to the baseball world. It wouldn't be for another 116 years [1994] that a similar retirement by a star Chicago baseball player would create such a commotion in the city.

Peter Golenbock
author,
referring to the retirements of
Spalding and Ryne Sandberg

In 1897 the 46-year-old [Cap] Anson announced that this would be his final year as an active player. On July 18, the skipper collected his 3,000th hit, the first man in baseball history to attain what was to become a benchmark achievement for future big-league hitters.

Donald Honig

Adrian "Cap" Anson

For nearly 30 years Anson has stood among the foremost representatives of the national game—a popular hero whose name was more familiar on the lips of people than that of any statesman or soldier of his time. He possessed many of the qualities that make leaders of men. . . . Baseball owes him much, the public owes him something, and Chicago owes him more.

Chicago Tribune

at the time of Cap Anson's dismissal as the White Stockings' manager, in 1898

For those who had seen him play from 1876 to 1897, Anson was the automatic choice as the game's all-time first baseman. Not until the arrival of the sleek-fielding George Sisler and his .400 bat in the 1920s and then the lethal slugging of Lou Gehrig soon thereafter was Cap finally toppled from his pedestal.

Donald Honig

Next to Anson, Mike "King" Kelly was the most popular man on the team; he was, in fact, one of 19th-century baseball's most swashbuckling characters. The King's pictures decorated the walls of saloons, barbershops, and poolrooms all over the city. His dashing style, strong good looks, and infectious Irish wit charmed everyone. Mike was a familiar figure in the city's nightlife, in his expensive tailor-made suits, squiring beautiful women, never meeting a bottle he could not empty.

Donald Honig

Mike "King" Kelly, after his sale to Boston's Beaneaters at the end of the 1886 season.

Mike Kelly, who afterwards became famous in baseball annals as the $10,000 beauty, was a whole-souled, genial fellow, with a host of friends and but one enemy, that one being himself. . . . Money slipped through Mike's fingers as water slips through the meshes of a fisherman's net, and he was as fond of whiskey as any representative of the Emerald Isle, but just the same he was a great ballplayer and one that became greater than he then was before ceasing to wear a Chicago uniform. He was as good a batter as anybody and a great thrower, both from the catcher's position and from the field, more men being thrown out by him than by any other man that could be named.

Cap Anson

During the Chance Era, the Peerless Leader led the Cubs to victory 753 times and suffered only 379 losses in the process. He was 21–11 in World Series play. He batted .297 in 15 years as a Cub and still holds the season and career stolen-base records for a Cub. Chicago has never seen his equal.

Jim Langford

on first baseman Frank Chance (1898–1912), who performed in the dual role of player/manager from 1905 to 1912

When he was given the opportunity to work behind the bat, he stopped the pitched balls with the ends of his fingers, the foul tips with his knees, and the wild pitches with the top of his head.

Anonymous Chicago writer

on Frank Chance

Frank Chance

Though he was hit in the head 36 times by pitched balls and finally had to have a brain operation, no pitcher ever succeeded in making him back away from the plate.

Peter Golenbock
on Chance

Injuries limited Frank Chance to 87 at-bats in 1911, and frequent beanings drove him to the hospital for an operation to remove blood clots in his brain at the end of the 1912 season.

Doug Myers

Johnny Evers was a nonstop chatterbox on the field, to the extent that both Chance and Tinker sometimes wished he was in the outfield.

Donald Honig

Johnny Evers

Most memorable of the [1906–08] pitchers was Mordecai "Three-Finger" Brown, a 20-game winner six straight years.

Sheldon Mix

The Giants were overcome by "Three-Finger" Brown, who finished the first game for Overall and pitched the whole second game. The only thing for Manager McGraw to do to beat Chicago is to dig up a pitcher with only two fingers.

Anonymous New York sportswriter

on Brown's crucial double-header win over the Giants, September 22, 1908, the day before the infamous "Merkle Boner" kept the Cubs alive in the pennant race

Philip K. Wrigley was a name synonymous with baseball ownership, the way Mack was in Philadelphia; Comiskey, with the Chicago White Sox; Yawkey, in Boston; Griffith, in Washington and Minnesota; and Stoneham, in New York and San Francisco.

Donald Honig

He had generally been popular with his players; his approaches to improving his team had not always been the correct ones, but they had been genuine and generous. Because he wanted to retain the aesthetics of Wrigley Field and had been concerned with the nocturnal tranquility of the surrounding neighborhood, he was the last holdout against night ball in his park. Not everyone agreed, but Wrigley's reasons were understood and respected.

Donald Honig
on Philip K. Wrigley

Grover Cleveland Alexander

NATIONAL BASEBALL HALL OF FAME LIBRARY, COOPERSTOWN, N.Y.

Early in Gabby Hartnett's career, the Cubs were playing the Reds. Pitching for the Reds was Carl Mays, the guy who killed Ray Chapman with a pitched ball. Mays had a reputation for knocking down batters; he was rough and mean. Hartnett came up, and Mays threw his underhand fastball that literally turned the peak of Hartnett's cap around. Nobody said anything, but the next time Mays came up to bat, Grover Cleveland Alexander slowly walked off the mound and up to home plate. He said, "Mays, I haven't made up my mind which eye I'm going to hit you in. Do you have a preference?" Mays pleaded with him. Whenever Alexander pitched, Mays was careful not to throw too close to Cubs batters.

Ed Froelich

Cubs employee who began work for the club in 1924 as the visiting team's batboy and later worked for manager Joe McCarthy

Hack Wilson

The way Alex pitched, you rarely saw his great stuff until it meant something. You'd see mediocre stuff, until he needed that extra.

Ed Froelich
on Grover Cleveland Alexander

Size 6 spikes, size 18 collar, and 200 pounds of solid muscle on a 5'6" frame, Hack Wilson terrorized NL pitchers with his oversized shillelagh.

Warren N. Wilbert
author

What are you going to do with a guy who, after being admonished for visiting Al Capone's box at Wrigley Field, says: "Well, he comes to our place, why shouldn't I go to his?"

Mark Kram
on Hack Wilson

Gabby Hartnett

Gabby [Hartnett] was a great guy, but he was a tough loser. That's why they called him Gabby—he was always yakking, pep talks. I'd like to see more of that today.

Phil Cavarretta

He was frank to the point of being cruel and as subtle as a belch.

Lee Allen

sportswriter,
on Rogers Hornsby

I'm a tough guy, a gambler on horses, a slave driver, and in general a disgrace to the game. I wish I knew why. I only wanted to win.

Rogers Hornsby

His first two years in the league, he couldn't get a hit off me. So he set out to methodically figure me out. He did it. From 1933 on, I couldn't get him out.

Carl Hubbell

New York Giants Hall of Fame pitcher, on seven-time NL All-Star second baseman Billy Herman (1931–41)

He never was very fast. And he only had a fair arm. But he was a brimful of batting and fielding talent, hustle, spirit, and—most of all—brains. He was, as the players say, a professional.

Tim Cohane

sportswriter/author, on Billy Herman

He should have been fired in 1951 for not using a fixed pitching rotation, but instead, it was the sight of him reading a novel in the dugout in the Polo Grounds that ended his tenure.

Doug Myers

on Cubs manager (1949–51) and former Cardinals Gashouse Gang star Frankie Frisch

I was all business as a player. I really focused on what was happening that day on the field. Now I have a much broader look at the game of baseball. It's fun to be a part of it, and fun to be in that dugout.

Ryne Sandberg

on his post-playing-career duties as a spring training instructor for the Cubs in Arizona

NATIONAL BASEBALL HALL OF FAME LIBRARY, COOPERSTOWN, N.Y.

Ryne Sandberg

One day I thought he was one of the best players in the National League. The next day I think he's one of the best players I've ever seen. He's Baby Ruth.

Whitey Herzog
St. Louis Cardinals manager (1980–90), on Sandberg

Everyone called him "The Natural" because of how easy he made things look on the baseball field. He was a natural, but he worked at it. He was as big an instigator on our team as anybody, but he did it in a very quiet manner. Even though he was at the top of his profession, he continued to work hard, like he was trying to win a job.

Larry Bowa
shortstop (1982–85), on Ryne Sandberg

Billy Williams

He was the "Quiet Hero." About the only thing he ever got his name in the newspapers for was winning a game with his bat or saving a game with his glove, as he did for Ken Holtzman's no-hitter in 1969.

Raymond Coffey

journalist,
on Billy Williams

Billy Williams had the best swing I ever saw in baseball.

Ferguson Jenkins

Hall of Fame pitcher (1966–73,
1982–83), 1971 National League
Cy Young Award winner

My arm has never felt better. When I have my uniform on, it thinks it's 25.

Ferguson Jenkins
at age 39

Fergie had tremendous control. I could almost catch him with a pair of pliers.

Randy Hundley
catcher (1966–73, 1976–77)

The first of the four consecutive Cy Young Awards won by Greg Maddux came in his last season in Chicago. At 26, he came into his own, winning a league-leading 20 games with a microscopic 2.18 ERA, threw four shutouts, and fielded his position flawlessly. To say any more is simply painful.

Doug Myers

The Cubs failed to sign their budding star after the 1992 season, losing him through free agency to Atlanta.

Just saying the name was fun: The *S*'s slid off your tongue like kids down a waterpark slide. *Ssssammmy Ssssosssa.*

Skip Bayless

sports journalist

I saw in Sammy the natural talent come out very early. He was, to me, a physical specimen and probably needed to work on his uncontrolled aggression at the plate, but he had the strong arm and he had the mechanics that probably needed a little seasoning, but I saw a lot of potential there.

Andre Dawson

on Sammy Sosa

Sammy Sosa

Watching Sosa unleash on a fat pitch was like watching a panther spring on its prey. You could almost see the teeth in Sosa's bat.

Skip Bayless

I think Sammy Sosa's the best. He reacts so well, blowing the kisses and everything. Every time I turn on a sports show with highlights, there's Sammy. . . . Sammy is so much fun. A couple times, he got so involved in the game he forgot to blow his mother a kiss, so I had the camera guy get the batboy to run over to get Sammy so he could do it.

Arne Harris

longtime WGN-TV director of Cubs broadcasts

I've seen the film of the game against Houston. I can't believe it's me. . . . That particular day, I was getting the calls, I was getting the breaks. A lot of luck was on my side. Everything had to work a certain way. Guys were swinging at bad pitches. I was getting borderline calls. The control was just there. I can't explain it. It pretty much came out of nowhere.

Kerry Wood

on his 20-K game against the Astros, May 6, 1998, tying the major league record for most strikeouts in a game, twice set by Roger Clemens

6

SHRINE TO
NO. 14

ERNIE BANKS, "MR. CUB," was one of
those great players who was cursed to
play out his career with an inferior team.
It is no exaggeration to say that the dif-
ference between an Ernie Banks and a
Mickey Mantle is the good fortune to
play with a championship team. Still,
there was something about him that
even opponents' fans applauded.

**Brendan C. Boyd and
Fred C. Harris**

The only thing that Ernie Banks and Hack Wilson had in common was the fact that neither ever refused to sign an autograph.

Mark Kram

In 1957 Banks was knocked down four times by four different pitchers—Don Drysdale, Bob Purkey, Bob Friend, and Jack Sanford. And each time he was knocked down, Banks hit their next pitch out of the park.

Tom Gorman
major league umpire (1951–76)

Banks was built like a letter opener, comported himself in the manner of a man applying for a loan, and relished his work; the only thing he disliked about playing two games was that he could not play three.

Mark Kram

Welcome to the friendly confines of Wrigley Field. Oh, oh, it's great to be alive and a Cub on this beautiful sun-kissed afternoon.

Ernie Banks

Conjure up all the sonnets, all the treacle that propagandists and the sentimental have contributed to the glorification of The Grand Old Game, and that is Ernie.

Mark Kram

He's a hundred billboards on a hundred highways. He's priceless as advertising.

Frank Lane

onetime White Sox, Cardinals, and Indians GM

My main target throughout my baseball career was to win the World Series of life, of living. That's really winning.

Ernie Banks

For nine years at shortstop and 10 more at first base, Banks, despite the oft-heard complaint that he couldn't hit in the clutch [though as Willie Mays noted about a similar complaint directed at another player, Ted Williams, you don't drive in 1,636 runs, as Banks did, without coming through in the clutch *once* in a while!], delighted not only Cub fans but fans in every city in which his team played.

Barry Gifford

Ernie swings a bat like Joe Louis used to throw a punch—short and sweet.

Clyde McCullough
catcher (1940–43, 1946–48, 1953–56)

He's got a helluva pair of forearms and wrists. You grab hold of him and it's like grabbing a piece of steel.

Bob Scheffing
catcher (1941–42, 1946–50)/
manager (1957–59),
on Ernie Banks

He gave Chicago what he had, foot down on the gas, every day.

Mark Kram

on Banks

His spirit is indestructible, and you always know baseball is near when Banks, like the geese honking north, almost every year predicts unflinchingly that the Cubs will win the pennant.

Mark Kram

If everybody loved baseball, if all the kids played it, there would be no shooting in the world.

Ernie Banks

What exemplifies the attitude of the Cub fan is Ernie Banks. Twenty-six and a half games out of first place, and he walks out of the dugout, looks around Wrigley Field, and says, "What a great day. Let's play two." Only a Cub fan could understand that.

Tom Dreesen

Talking was not a big part of our lives when I first came here. I got that from Jackie Robinson. First time I walked on the field, he came across over to third base, and he said, "I'm glad to see you here, and I know you can make it. You've got a lot of ability. Just listen." And that's what I did.

Ernie Banks

Many of the players didn't quite understand my own philosophy. I believe in forgive and forget, and keep your mouth shut and listen to whatever somebody is trying to tell you and you can learn something. I tell my children that. But it was just misinterpreted that Leo [Durocher] disliked me. He made my life better, he made me a better player.

Ernie Banks

The only real sore point of the '59 season occurred when the Cubs were not even on the field. It happened after the season was over, during the pennant playoff between L.A. and Milwaukee. Ed Mathews hit a home run in a losing cause, his 46th of the year, which gave him the championship by one over Ernie Banks, with whom he'd ended the regular season in a tie. Banks was not afforded the opportunity to play in any extra games, and so had what would have been his share of a second consecutive crown unfairly snatched from him. Banks and Mathews both ended their careers with 512 home runs, but to me, because of that extra shot by Mathews, Banks takes precedence on the all-time list.

Barry Gifford

The old saying "Things even out in the end" may hold true here. While much has been made of the Mathews playoff advantage, a little-known fact is that on June 18, 1958, Mathews hit a home run that was wiped out because the game was called after one and a half innings on account of rain. The Braves' foe that day? The Cubs, of course.

It's been an education. I look at Wrigley Field as really a university for me, learning about different kinds of people, different cultures, different philosophies.

Ernie Banks

Embarrassment and unkind things that we all must learn from really can make us better—better people, better individuals.

Ernie Banks

"Let's play two." That started in '69. Like most things, it just kind of came out. It was July and over 100 degrees, and everybody was kind of down a little bit. I came in the locker room, and Jimmy Enright was there and a lot of writers were around, and I said, "Boy, this is a great day. Let's play two."

Ernie Banks

7

MAJOR MOMENTS

AFTER THE 1888 SEASON, Cap Anson took his club and a team of "All-Americans" on baseball's first world tour. Designed to bring America's game to the shores of the Old World, the teams played in the capitals of Europe and went as far as Cairo, where a game was played in the shadows of the pyramids.

Donald Honig

When manager Frank Chance led the Chicago Cubs team into New York the morning of October 8, 1908, to meet the Giants that afternoon to settle a tie for the National League pennant, I had a half-dozen "black hand" letters in my coat pocket. "We'll kill you," these letters said, "if you pitch and beat the Giants."

Mordecai Peter Centennial "Three-Finger" Brown
Hall of Fame pitcher (1904–12, 1916)

Brown and the Cubs beat New York, 4–2, in one of the most famous playoff games in major league history. The two teams ended the 1908 season deadlocked, forcing a playoff. The game might not have been played had there not been a controversial ending to an earlier Giants-Cubs game, on September 23. In that contest, with two out in the bottom of the ninth, runners at the corners, and the score tied, Al Bridwell singled to bring in the apparent winning run. However, Fred Merkle, the runner at first, failed to touch second base, turning instead toward the clubhouse to avoid hordes of jubilant fans who rushed onto the Polo Grounds field. Johnny Evers retrieved a baseball (perhaps the game ball—in the confusion no one was sure), signaled umpire Bob Emslie, and stepped on second base, forcing Merkle and erasing the run. With the crush of fans precluding further play, the Cubs claimed victory by forfeit. League officials ultimately ruled Merkle out, and the game ended in a 1–1 tie, setting the stage for the October 8 playoff.

Today a multitude of men are bewailing the gruesome fact that Merkle did not run to second in that tie game. That omission cost New York the pennant. It was a common error, the slovenly heedlessness that keeps most of mankind in its rut, and exalts the men who play the game, be it business, or love, or war, to the bitter end.

**New York American
editorial page**
October 9, 1908

I suppose when I die, they'll put on my tombstone, "Here lies Bonehead Merkle."

Fred Merkle

New York Giants infielder during the aforementioned 1908 blunder and later a Chicago Cubs first baseman (1917–20)

Merkle's blunder cost New York the pennant. True. This does not lower the price of beef; it does not make travel on the Third Avenue "L" any less hazardous; it does not save the old from toil or the poor from hunger. It affects not one jot the status of any of the hundreds of thousands who were wrought up over the victory that has been borne away to Chicago.

New York American editorial page
October 9, 1908

The game will never know another battle like that of 1908.

John McGraw

former New York Giants manager, before he died in 1934, on the NL playoff game, October 8, 1908, won by the Cubs, 4–2

New York had the game won until the third inning, in which Joe Tinker was Chicago's first batter. Christy Mathewson feared Tinker, and he signaled [Cy] Seymour to play deep in center field. He was afraid that a long drive by Tinker might turn the tide of battle. Seymour saw the signal but disregarded it. Matty dropped his famous "fade away" over the plate, and Tinker drove a long, high fly to left center. Seymour made a desperate effort to reach the ball but fell a few feet short. The ball rolled to the crowd in the outfield for a three-base hit and started a rally that gave Chicago the victory.

Johnny Evers

*second baseman (1902–13)/
manager (1913, 1921),
on the October 8, 1908, show-
down between New York and
Chicago for the National League
pennant, won by the Cubs, 4–2*

Joe Tinker

Of all those who played baseball at the time, Joe Tinker was the only one the great Christy Mathewson couldn't take charge of when the pressure was on. The Cubs' shortstop hit Matty as if he owned him.

Warren Brown
sports journalist/author

On June 28, 1910, Joe Tinker became the first man to steal home twice in one game, as the Cubs beat Cincinnati in Chicago, 11–1.

Warren N. Wilbert

On July 19, 1909, in New York City, National League President Harry Pulliam committed suicide. Since the end of the 1908 season he had taken a leave of absence from his job, because of a severe state of depression, which his doctors said had been brought on by the turmoil that followed the Giant-Cub game of September 23, 1908.

G.H. Fleming
author

In his first at-bat of the 1924 season, against the Giants, Cub shortstop Charlie Hollocher drilled a shot over first base that hit fair and then curved foul, directly into a hole along the right-field grandstand. While New York right fielder Ross Youngs was frantically digging for it, the Cubs' midfielder circled the bases for an inside- *and* outside-the-park dinger.

Warren N. Wilbert

The Series of 1929 was marked by Hack Wilson losing Mule Haas's fly ball in the sun for a bargain-basement homer while the [Philadelphia] Athletics were engineering a 10-run inning against the Cubs. Wilson's blunder earned him a niche with Heinie Zimmerman, Johnny Miljus, Mickey Owen, and similar Series goats.

David Condon
Chicago Tribune, *May 23, 1972*

The Cubs' unusual Series of 1932 also featured Babe Ruth, by then a Yankee and Sultan of Swat. Ruth made that Series historical by signaling—to pitcher Charlie Root and 49,986 Wrigley Field fans—exactly when and where he would deliver a home run. A Cub player said, "We were lucky we weren't killed."

David Condon
Chicago Tribune, *May 23, 1972*

There has always been some question as to whether Babe Ruth *did* call his shot, his final World Series home run, and to whom he was pointing. The bleacher bum version is that he was pointing to a black man named Amos "Loudmouth" Latimer, traveling secretary for the Chicago Negro League's 47th Street team. The story, which Loudmouth told for years afterward, goes that Latimer had been provoking Ruth from the center-field bleachers by throwing lemon rinds at him and calling him "brother," a reference Ruth had heard before because of his facial features and the fact that he was an orphan. Ruth finally turned around and, from the field, told Loudmouth he had one coming. The next inning he deposited Charlie Root's delivery a few feet away from Amos.

E. M. Swift
writer/author

My first game, September 25, 1934, was the highest, most thrilling moment I ever had. I was just 18 years old. We were playing Cincinnati. The pitcher was Whitey Wistert—when you do something good against a guy, you remember. It was 0–0 going into the seventh inning. I wasn't a home run hitter. I was like Mark Grace. I hit a home run and we won, 1–0.

Phil Cavarretta

It was very dark by then. . . . I swung with everything I had and then I got that feeling you get when the blood rushes out of your head and you get dizzy. A lot of people have told me they didn't know the ball was in the bleachers. Well I did—maybe I was the only one in the park who did. I knew it the minute I hit it. When I got to second base I couldn't see third for the players and fans there. . . . That was the shot that did it. We went into first place. And while we still had the pennant to win, we couldn't be headed.

Gabby Hartnett

Hall of Fame catcher (1922–40), on his infamous "Homer in the Gloamin'," September 28, 1938, that beat Pittsburgh, 6–5

In the 1945 World Series, the Cubs won three games, matching their victory total in four previous Series appearances since losing to Boston and Babe Ruth in 1918.

David Condon
Chicago Tribune, *May 22, 1972*

Thanks to nifty hurling by Hank Borowy and Claude Passeau, and some weird English on Stan Hack's bounding double in game No. 6, the Cubs achieved three thrilling triumphs [in the 1945 World Series]. As James Thurber suggested in his equally improbable story of the baseball midget, you could look it up.

David Condon
Chicago Tribune, *May 23, 1972*

Thurber's short story "You Could Look It Up" appeared in The Saturday Evening Post *in 1941, predating longtime Cubs employee and St. Louis Browns/Chicago White Sox owner Bill Veeck's life-imitates-art publicity stunt in 1951, when he signed midget Eddie Gaedel to a one-game contract with the Browns.*

Claude William Passeau consistently had posted twin-figure victory totals in the six seasons since the Cubs grabbed him from the Phillies. . . . Now Passeau neared his finest hour. Just 28 Tigers faced him. Rudy York's second-inning single was Detroit's only hit. Bob Swift drew Passeau's sole walk and was a double-play victim. It was the most spectacular World Series pitching performance in history up to that point.

David Condon

Chicago Tribune, *May 23, 1972, on Passeau's Game 3 win at Detroit in the 1945 World Series*

I just took my eyes off the ball and it hit me on the ring finger on my right hand. It swoll up and I couldn't hold the ball. If it hadn't been for that sixth game, I think we would've won. I tried to pitch like that, and it was just like pitching batting practice. I still believe we would've won the Series.

Claude Passeau

on the injury he sustained off the bat of Detroit's Jimmy Outlaw in the seventh inning of Game 6 of the 1945 World Series. Leading 5–1 at the time, the Cubs held on to take an 8–7 win in the 12th. Passeau also hurled a shutout in Game 3 of the '45 Series

To me, it was the saddest moment of my life. That particular play lost us the ball game. I was really upset. But I caught the ball. In those days, there was no TV. There was no replay. But I know definitely I caught the ball in the pocket of my glove.

Andy Pafko

center fielder/third baseman (1943–51), on the "home run in a glove," April 30, 1949, against the St. Louis Cardinals. What would have been a game-ending, diving catch by Pafko and a Cubs victory was ruled a trapped ball by umpire Al Barlick. As the two argued the play, two Cardinals runners scored, handing the Cubs a 4–3 defeat

On February 15, 1964, Ken Hubbs and a companion were killed in a plane crash near Provo, Utah. Hubbs, who had recently received his pilot's license, was flying home to Colton, California. Taking off in his Cessna 172 in what were described as unfavorable weather conditions [visibility was three miles], they crashed through the ice of Utah Lake moments after becoming airborne.

Donald Honig

In 1962 [Lou] Brock batted .263, flashed some dazzling speed, and on June 27 became the second player ever to smash one into the center-field bleachers at the Polo Grounds [temporary home of the Mets], a ride of some 500 feet.

Donald Honig

Nobody could figure it out, because we all knew that Lou was going to be a star.

Don Elston

on the Cubs' trade of Lou Brock to the Cardinals in mid-season 1964

It was one of those days where fate smiles on you. I didn't strike out anyone, and I don't think I walked too many guys either. . . . Aaron's ball blew a little toward the foul line, and it finally came down where that little recess is where the wall curves and Billy [Williams] stuck his glove up and caught it. You think the gods must be looking in on the game. I've always said a no-hitter is just a well-pitched game with a lot of luck.

Ken Holtzman

on his August 19, 1969, no-hitter against Atlanta at Wrigley Field

It was a big game for us, really. I remember that day because the wind was blowing in a ton. You wouldn't think you could hit a ball out. I'd thrown [Willie] Stargell a couple of strikes. I threw him a pitch that, to me, was not a bad pitch, but it was low and in. He hit a line drive up into right field, and you know, whenever he hit it, it was gone. . . . We should've pitched him away, with the way the wind was blowing like it was. It was a big game because we were at home, and we always won at home, and then we were going to Shea Stadium.

Phil Regan

pitcher (1968–72),
on what many feel was the turning point of the 1969 season, a critical extra-inning home loss to the Pirates on September 7. Regan was one strike away from victory when Stargell hit his game-tying shot out onto Sheffield Avenue

The noises of the day—the deep, happy roaring of the fans; the ancient, carny-show strains of the Wrigley Field organ [sometimes playing upbeat old airs like Cole Porter's "From This Moment On"] —seemed to reach us with a washed and wonderful clarity. . . . It was as if the entire baseball season—all those hundreds of games and thousands of innings—had happened, just this one time, in order to bring this afternoon to pass: a championship game and the Cubs.

Roger Angell

on the opening game of the 1984 National League Championship Series, Chicago vs. San Diego, won by the Cubs, 13–0

I don't have to fade back too far as to what I did to help this ball club win. I believe I played 140-something games that year; I had some aggressive power numbers. My average was good, my RBIs were good. But sometimes you have people who want to try and judge you on a certain play. It's a shame.

Leon "Bull" Durham

*first baseman (1981–88),
on the ground ball that slipped
through his legs, allowing the
tying run to score in the fifth and
deciding game of the National
League Championship Series loss
to San Diego in 1984*

I don't put my ground ball in '84 on the same level as the Buckner deal. We still had innings to go. That was it for him. . . . It wasn't for us, and I can accept that. If I had a problem with that, I wouldn't be in uniform today. I'd be somewhere hiding out.

Leon Durham

Being able to pitch at Wrigley Field was pretty awesome, but also being able to pitch against my idol I think was the ultimate. I came out of the game with a lead, and we held on and won, so it was a great day. I was able to have my first major league start and win it, and on the other side of the field beat Steve Carlton, so it was a very, very memorable day.

Jamie Moyer
pitcher (1986–88)

San Francisco's pitcher, Roger Mason, sent a one-hopper into right field, but [Andre] Dawson, not conceding the single, fielded it and threw a 90-mile-an-hour fastball that beat Mason to first base by a step and a half. It was something I'd never seen before. . . . In the sixth, Dawson tripled to complete [hitting for the] cycle. It was a rare thing—the second thing he'd done in the game that I'd never seen before.

Lonnie Wheeler

at a Cubs-Giants game,
April 1987

"Let there be light," proclaimed the longest-suffering Cubs fan, 91-year-old Harry Grossman, in a biblical voice. The Cubs' holiest relics, Ernie Banks and Billy Williams, threw out first balls. Chicago's most sentimental pitcher, Rick Sutcliffe, took the mound. "It's almost like sunshine and Wrigley are saying goodbye to each other," he thought. Looking hard at the Phillies' leadoff man, Phil Bradley, and straight into a light show of Instamatic flashes, Sutcliffe was struck by history—and Bradley. A home run right off the bat, the perfect note played on a party horn.

Tom Callahan

Time, *August 22, 1988,*
on the first baseball game
played under the lights at Wrigley
Field, August 8, 1988, a contest
postponed by rain after three and
a half innings

Jerome Walton, the leadoff man the team had needed, ran up a 30-game hitting streak [1989], the longest by a Cub in the modern era, breaking Ron Santo's 28-game run [1966].

Donald Honig

Outfielder Walton (1989–92) was selected National League Rookie of the Year in '89, the first Cub to be so honored since Kenny Hubbs in 1962.

It wasn't easy. One-hundred twenty-three games. Actually, the error that happened came in the Astrodome. It was a shot that came off of Mark Grace's glove, and I came over and got down on my knees and made the play, ending up on my stomach. The guy beat it out at first, but the ball trickled away. There was a guy on first, who went from first to second, and then he went from second to third on the error. That was the error that ended the streak. There was a lot of attention during that streak toward the end, so I was kind of happy when it ended.

Ryne Sandberg

on his major league-record 123-game errorless streak, fielding more chances without error by any infielder ever, other than first basemen, from June 21, 1989, to May 17, 1990

That play was the key for us.

Luis Castillo

Florida Marlins second baseman, who hit the catchable fly ball touched by Cubs fan Steve Bartman that led to one of the greatest collapses in sports history. With the Cubs leading, 3–0, and just five outs from their first World Series appearance since 1945, Castillo and the Marlins were given new life when Bartman's interference prevented Cubs left fielder Moises Alou from recording the second out of the eighth inning of Game 6 of the 2003 NLCS. The gaffe led to an eight-run inning by the Marlins, and the Cubs squandered another lead the following night to continue their staggering tradition of misfortune

That ball's gotta go. It's like the ring from *The Lord of the Rings* and we're kind of like Frodo, trying to get it over with. It will be destroyed in a way that there is a mess.

Grant DePorter

co-purchaser of the famed Bartman Ball, sold at auction for $113,824

The baseball was then handed over to Oscar-winning demolition expert Michael Lantieri, who blew up the ball before a large gathering in front of the late Harry Caray's downtown Chicago restaurant. The ball, according to an Associated Press account, received "VIP treatment in its last hours, from a farewell trip to Wrigley and a last night on public display in a hotel suite to a final 'dinner' of prime steak and lobster and even a massage."

In a flash, the ball that came to symbolize the Chicago Cubs' cursed history was blown up Thursday night, reduced to a pile of thread by a Hollywood special effects expert. Hundreds of fans sang "Take Me Out to the Ball Game" before the ball—the foul fly touched by Steve Bartman in last October's playoffs—was obliterated.

The Associated Press
February 26, 2004

I think it's very appropriate; it's symbolic of a new beginning.

Rachel Cannon

Cubs fan, on the demolition of the "cursed" Bartman Ball, February 26, 2004, in downtown Chicago

8

CHICAGO CUBS ALL-TIME TEAM

As LONG-ESTEEMED CHICAGO SPORTS journalist/author Warren Brown said in 1946, "Any attempt to rank the 803 personages who have drawn Chicago National League baseball paychecks at one time or another obviously must lead to argument."

Let the jawing begin. For your scrutinous review and argumentative pleasure: the Chicago Cubs All-Time Team.

If there was a Mr. Cub of the 19th century, surely it was Cap Anson. . . . In 22 years with Chicago, he rapped 3,041 hits for a .334 lifetime average. As a manager, he led his charges to five championships in his first eight tries.

Jim Langford

ADRIAN "CAP" ANSON
First base (1876–97)

Anson, the first major leaguer to reach 3,000 lifetime hits, still holds the National League record for most seasons batting over .300 (19). Using a split grip on the bat, Anson captured four batting titles and eight RBI crowns. Only three times in his 22 seasons with the White Stockings did he fail to hit .300 or more.

As a manager, he is credited with instituting the rotation of pitchers, but baseball's greatest 19th-century player cannot escape the shameful legacy of influencing the barring of black players from the game, the repercussions of which were painfully felt until 1947.

His 1,282 wins as the Cubs' pilot exceeds the club's No. 2 manager of all time by more than 300 victories.

I saw them all. . . . I saw all the best second basemen who ever played, and in my opinion, Ryne Sandberg is the best second baseman who ever played baseball.

Don Zimmer

manager (1988–91)

RYNE SANDBERG
Second base (1982–94, 1996–97)

Sandberg rewrote the definition of the definitive second baseman originally delineated by Eddie Collins, onetime Cub Rogers Hornsby, Napoleon Lajoie, Jackie Robinson, and Joe Morgan.

No one out-hit Hornsby, but Sandberg produced showy offensive totals that also included power (a league-leading 40 home runs in 1990). His defensive consistency at the keystone spot is unrivaled: He is the only man in history ever to win nine consecutive Gold Glove awards at his position.

A former *Parade* High School All-America quarterback, Sandberg, the 1984 NL MVP and a 10-time All-Star, set the all-time major league mark for most consecutive games without an error by not only a second baseman but all infield positions excepting first base (123).

He was out there every day, hurt or not; he had marvelous instincts, and he could hit.

Billy Williams

on Ron Santo

RON SANTO
Third base (1960–73)

He was the Cubs' captain and cleanup hitter, an inspirational, heel-clicking catalyst who endeared himself to Cubs fans and alienated opponents.

Santo, a nine-time All-Star, was the National League's premier third baseman during the 1960s, a consistent run producer who was underrated in the field.

While Cooperstown has embarrassingly shunned Santo's merits, Chicagoans know his worth. He banged out 337 homers and batted .279 during 14 years in Wrigleyville. He holds the all-time record for most seasons leading the majors in total fielding chances (nine).

He is—well, mustard on a kid's face, Babe Ruth promising a home run to a boy in the hospital, the smell of spring and an old, cracking boyhood glove, and all those memories and moments and everything that is a symbol of America.

Mark Kram

on Ernie Banks

ERNIE BANKS
Shortstop (1953–71)

Everything Cubbie is embodied in Banks. The first back-to-back National League MVP (1958, '59), he is the soul of what baseball is all about. But his unrivaled enthusiasm, as superb as it was, pales next to his lengthy list of on-field accomplishments.

The Hall of Famer, Mr. Cub, recorded 512 career home runs, leading the league twice—something shortstops just did not do before he came along—and still owns the NL mark for most round-trippers by a shortstop in a single season (47, set in 1958). Three times he led league shortstops in fielding.

The slightly built Banks's source of power was always a mystery. Asked if, as a child, he ate his spinach, like Popeye, Banks replied: "Yeah, I did. Cabbage, too. I didn't smoke a pipe, though, and my girlfriend wasn't named Olive Oyl."

Hartnett was so good that he lasted 20 years in spite of the fact that he couldn't run. All other skills were refined in him, and the greatest of these was his throwing. Squatting behind home plate, he could whistle the ball down to second base on a trajectory as flat as his feet.

Red Smith

legendary sports journalist

GABBY HARTNETT
Catcher (1922–40)

The 1935 National League MVP, Hartnett is a legend for his "Homer in the Gloamin'," struck in the waning twilight against the Pirates in late September of 1938. The wallop gave the Cubs a half-game lead over Pittsburgh that they never relinquished.

Hartnett sparkled defensively, too, leading National League receivers six times in fielding percentage. He possessed a rifle throwing arm and caught over 100 games a season 12 times. Hartnett also collected over 200 victories as a Cubs manager, from 1938 to '40.

En route to training camp as a rookie in 1922, the quiet Charles Leo Hartnett was nicknamed "Gabby" by a reporter.

The first time you saw him, you said, "Here's a star." He had so much power. When he hit the ball, it was like a rifle shot.

Don Elston

pitcher (1953, 1957–64), on Billy Williams

BILLY WILLIAMS
Left field (1959–74)

The durable, sweet-swinging Williams, the Cubs' quiet left fielder, was a clutch performer who once held the National League record for most consecutive games played —1,117. For consistency, Williams connected on 20 or more home runs a year for 13 straight seasons.

The six-time All-Star was 1961 NL Rookie of the Year and led the league in batting (.333) in 1972, the same year he was selected *The Sporting News*' Player of the Year. He also led the league in hits (205) in 1970 and runs (137, also in '70).

Pirates Hall of Fame slugger Willie Stargell once referred to Williams's compact swing as "poetry in motion."

I never saw a guy win games the way he did that year. We never lost a game all year if he came up in the late innings with a chance to get a hit that would win it for us. . . . No tougher player ever lived than Hack Wilson.

Joe McCarthy
manager (1926–30),
on Hack Wilson's 1930 season

HACK WILSON
Center field (1926–31)

The colorful Wilson had a brilliant if turbulent six years in Cubbieland, topped by his phenomenal 1930 season, in which he set the still-standing major league record for most RBIs in a single season, an astronomical 191, while belting 56 round-trippers.

If ever a player had an MVP year, it was Wilson in '30. But strangely, mirroring the misfortune that often dogged him, most of it of Wilson's own making, there was no MVP award given that year.

In his first three seasons with the club, the power-hitting Wilson led the National League in home runs. But the heavy drinking that saturated his playing days ultimately curtailed his major league career and eventually killed him at age 48.

The most obvious thing that carried us was the phenomenon that was Sammy Sosa. He was unbelievable. What he did was not only hit all these home runs that were winning ball games and always making us feel like we could win the ball games, but so much of the attention was on Sammy that it allowed other people to just go to work. Sammy had a huge media responsibility every day. He handled it with a smile on his face and got his work in.

Jim Riggleman
manager (1995–99)

SAMMY SOSA
Right field (1992–)

Though 1998 will always be his defining year, when he battled Mark McGwire to the wire as both smashed Roger Maris's 37-year-old single-season home run record, Sosa, a beloved fan favorite, has shown a consistency worthy of an all-time team selection.

Right field in Wrigley has offered a few all-time team candidates over the years, most notably Andre Dawson, Kiki Cuyler, and Wildfire Schulte.

Sosa's clutch hitting produced nine straight 100-RBI seasons through 2003, and he surpassed Mr. Cub, the immortal Banks, in lifetime Cubs home runs, in 2004. He is the only man in major league history to hit 60 or more home runs in a season three times.

He may have lost that classic home run race in '98, but it was Sosa who came away with the league MVP award that year, the 10th time a Cub had been so honored.

A farm accident when Brown was seven years old mangled his right hand. When he tried pitching, he found his disfigured digits put an unhittable spin on the ball. . . . Ty Cobb called Brown's curve "the most devastating pitch I've ever faced."

Pete Cava

MORDECAI
"THREE-FINGER" BROWN
Pitcher (1904–12, 1916)

The Hall of Famer was the mainstay of the great Cubs clubs of 1906–10 that won four pennants and two World Series crowns (the Cubs' last), including the fabulous 1906 team that collected 116 wins—still the major league record for a single season.

Brown, nearly 90 years after he last pitched for Chicago, is still the club career leader in ERA (1.80), complete games (206), and shutouts (48). His 29 wins in 1908 are the most recorded by a Cubs pitcher in a single season, and his 188 career victories place No. 2 all-time behind Charlie Root.

Brown will forever be remembered for his classic duels with New York Giants immortal Christy Mathewson. In their 24 head-to-head meetings, Brown won 13, including nine in a row. He also won five World Series games.

As a manager, Chance played the kind of baseball that exemplified the dead-ball era. His strategy was to manufacture the one run that would win the ball game. . . . Chance relied on the steal and also, especially, the sacrifice. . . . He forgave errors, just as long as the players tried. But nobody could last with him if he pulled boneheaded plays or didn't hustle. You had to be able to take direction and execute to play on Frank Chance's Cubs.

Peter Golenbock

FRANK CHANCE
Manager (1905–12)

Chance, "the Peerless Leader," like Anson, was a player/manager, and also not unlike Anson, was an excellent first baseman.

While Anson logged more lifetime wins piloting the Cubs, it was Chance who guided the club through its Golden Age, fielding four National League champions and two world championship teams in his eight seasons as field boss. His .664 winning percentage tops all Cubs managers, including Anson and Albert Spalding.

A big man for his time, at six feet, 188 pounds, Chance surprisingly was a superb base stealer, and in fact is still the Cubs' career (402) and single-season leader (67) in thefts.

CUBS ALL-TIME TEAM

Cap Anson, *first base*

Ryne Sandberg, *second base*

Ron Santo, *third base*

Ernie Banks, *shortstop*

Gabby Hartnett, *catcher*

Billy Williams, *left field*

Hack Wilson, *center field*

Sammy Sosa, *right field*

Mordecai "Three-Finger" Brown,
pitcher

Frank Chance, *manager*

NATIONAL LEAGUE MVPs

1911   **Frank "Wildfire" Schulte**
(Chalmers Award)

1929   **Rogers Hornsby**

1935   **Gabby Hartnett**

1945   **Phil Cavarretta**

1952   **Hank Sauer**

1958   **Ernie Banks**

1959   **Ernie Banks**

1984   **Ryne Sandberg**

1987   **Andre Dawson**

1998   **Sammy Sosa**

Retired Cubs Numbers

10   **Ron Santo**, *third base* (1960–73)
—jersey retired: 2003

14   **Ernie Banks**, *shortstop/first base*
(1953–71)—jersey retired: 1982

26   **Billy Williams**, *left field* (1959–74)
—jersey retired: 1987

42   In honor of **Jackie Robinson**
—jersey retired: 1997

NL Rookies of the Year

1961   **Billy Williams**, *left field*

1962   **Ken Hubbs**, *second base*

1989   **Jerome Walton**, *outfield*

1998   **Kerry Wood**, *pitcher*

9

THE GREAT CUBS TEAMS

Y OU'VE GOT TO TRY to win 90-plus to win your division. That was our goal—which we did, but we ended up second. People don't remember second place, but in our case they do. It's just the mystique of being the Chicago Cubs. We were a second-place team people remember.

Ferguson Jenkins

on the 1969 Cubs

I was playing with the best ball team ever put together—The Chicagos of 1882. I bar no team in the world when I say that. I know about the New York Giants, the Detroits, and the Big Four, the 1886 St. Louis Browns and all of them, but they never were in it with the old 1882 gang that pulled down the pennant for Chicago.

Mike "King" Kelly
Hall of Fame catcher (1880–86)

When we marched on the field with our big six-footers out in front, it used to be a case of "eat 'em up, Jake." There were seven of us six feet high: Anson, Goldsmith, Dalrymple, Gore, Williamson, Flint, and myself being in that neighborhood. We had most of 'em whipped before we threw a ball. They were scared to death.

Mike "King" Kelly
*on the 1882 Chicago
White Stockings*

After winning 116 games in 1906—a major league record that still stands—the Cubs were rock-solid favorites to beat their South Side rivals, the White Sox, in the World Series. The Sox had won the American League pennant that year despite an anemic team batting average of .228 that earned them the nickname "Hitless Wonders." The Cubs players were so confident that before the opening game they discussed what kind of prize they'd choose after dispensing with the formality of beating the White Sox. But the "Hitless Wonders," refusing to be awed, calmly captured the Series, four games to two.

Sheldon Mix

A year later [1907], the Cubs' World Series opponent was Detroit, led at the plate by Ty Cobb and "Wahoo" Sam Crawford. Some quarters predicted that "Cobb alone will beat the Cubs." The Cubs . . . scored a four-game sweep after the first contest ended in a tie. Crawford could hit no better than .238 against the Cubs. Cobb, the American League batting champion, was held to .200.

Sheldon Mix

The Detroit Tigers repeated as American League champions in 1908, and in the World Series lost again to Chicago, this time four games to one. The Cubs thus became the first team to win the Series two years in a row.

Sheldon Mix

Frank Chance's Cubs have proven their title as the greatest aggregation ever gathered on a diamond, game, true, and loyal to the core.

Chicago News
October 9, 1908

During the 1927 season, the Cubs managed to win 15 extra-inning games, establishing a club record.

Warren N. Wilbert

Then came The Streak. Between September 4, 1935, when the Cubs were down 2½ games in the standings, and September 27, they reeled off 21 straight wins, absolutely astounding the baseball world, while knocking the Giants and Cardinals out of contention.

Warren N. Wilbert

In September we put on a real drive. We won 21 straight games. You ever go 75 miles an hour on the highway while everybody else is doing 50? That's how we felt.

Phil Cavarretta

on the 1935 NL champion Cubs

The Cubs would win just one pennant in the 1940s [1945], and then an entire generation of Chicago fans would gaze wistfully back as it receded into the past. It became like a last oasis on a trek that seemed to have no end. Half-pennants—division titles in 1984 and 1989—brought some measure of satisfaction, but the lone pennant of 1945 remained forlorn and beckoning, the gallant symbol of what was to some a lost empire.

Donald Honig

He [manager Charlie Grimm] liked to pitch me to death. Two days' rest, three days' rest. I relieved on the side. I think that's how come we won the pennant, all the pitching I did.

Hank Wyse

pitcher (1942–47), Game 2 loser in the 1945 World Series

I was so fortunate to come to the Cubs at a time when we had such great role models. I was a young guy. Beck [Glenn Beckert] and I came up the same year. We had guys like Ernie Banks and Billy Williams and Ron Santo and George Altman. These were great guys. Not just good players, but great guys. It was great for us to be around a group like that. . . . We stayed together for many years. That group really cared about each other. There was a unique relationship between the players and the fans with that group that in all my 16 years we were never able to emulate.

Don Kessinger
shortstop (1964–75),
on the 1965 Cubs, his first full
season with Chicago

In '69 we were close-knit. Everybody knew one another, because we started to play together in the early '60s. We had Billy, Ronnie, Ernie, Beckert and Kessinger, and then Hickman came on the scene. We got a chance to know one another. It was a very small clubhouse. We didn't make any money, so nobody was jealous of our salaries. We didn't make squat back in those days. I think everybody understood we were trying to win a championship for the Cubs and for the city.

Ferguson Jenkins

It was standing room only and we had just come off a trip. We had something like a seven- or eight-game lead, and we had been in first place most of the year. Cub fever was all over the city. You couldn't get through the crowd to park your car. It was absolutely packed. The people were yelling during batting practice, and Dick Selma was leading the bleacher bums. The whole atmosphere was kind of nuts.

Ken Holtzman

on the temperament around
Wrigley Field, August 1969

They smell the money.

Leo Durocher

on the '69 Cubs

For a while in 1969, it looked as if the Cubs were going to finally return to the postseason, but they ran out of gas and coasted to a halt in the path of divine intervention. They ended up as the most famous and most celebrated second-place team in the history of sports.

Doug Myers

Because we played our games early, we put pressure on the opposition by winning early. Once they looked up on the board, because of the day games, and saw that the Cubs had won, there was instant pressure.

Gary Matthews
on the 1984 Cubs

That was the most fun year of all time. We made it fun. Guys couldn't wait to get to the ballpark to be able to take batting practice. . . . I gave out hats, painter's caps, to the people in the left-field bleachers, and you could flip up the bill and they said "Sarge" on the cap. Whenever I would do something good, the people in the left-field stands would stand up, and when I saluted them they would sit down. . . . It was a great year, and a great year for baseball.

Gary "Sarge" Matthews
on the '84 Cubs

I was there in the spring, and they [the Cubs] had a lot of attention from the media. I mean, they're talking about going to the World Series. They've got a new attitude, lofty expectations—we'll see how they handle that.

Ryne Sandberg

on the 2004 Cubs at the start of the regular season

10

FIELDS
OF PLAY

THE YANKEES HAVE THEIR 39 pennants, their pin-stripes, and the Babe. The Red Sox have their Fenway Franks and their Green Monster. The Cardinals have their Clydesdales, the Royals their Dancing Waters, and the Padres their Chicken. And just about every team in the majors can lay claim to greater on-the-field success than the Cubs over the past four decades. But nobody, meaning nobody, has got what we've got: the best damn ballpark that ever was or ever will be, period.

**David Fulk and
Dan Riley**

The White Stockings played their first two years at a park called the 23rd Street Grounds, located not far from the Lake Michigan shore at State Street and 23rd. . . . In 1878 the White Stockings moved to a new home, Lakefront Park, located south of Randolph Street between Michigan Avenue and the Illinois Central tracks. The park was renovated and enlarged in 1883, increasing its capacity to 10,000—largest in the league. . . . The park even featured a forerunner of today's luxury boxes—eighteen rows of private boxes with curtains and armchairs.

Donald Honig

Because Lakefront Park had been built to dimensions dictated by certain real-estate constraints, its left-field fence was unusually close to home plate—according to some contemporary accounts, little more than 200 feet away. In the dead-ball era, outfield fences were not built as home run targets but as park enclosures, and most home runs were legged out inside the park. Any ball that took wing over it was a ground-rule double.

Donald Honig

In 1885 [the White Stockings] moved to their new home, West Side Park, located at Congress and Loomis Streets. The new arena featured a horseshoe-shaped grandstand with accommodations for 2,500 and a bleacher section with 3,500 seats. For the well-heeled, there were a dozen rooftop boxes furnished with individual chairs. A twelve-foot brick wall enclosed the outfield.

Donald Honig

The team's home during its world championship years was a shabby old ballpark at Polk and Wolcott, where County Hospital now stands. Best known of that era were the double-play threesome: shortstop Joe Tinker, second baseman Johnny Evers, and manager/first baseman Frank Chance, who were immortalized by Franklin P. Adams's famed poem that recited the line, "Tinker to Evers to Chance."

Sheldon Mix

Going to the Cubs Park was adventuresome because I rode the Clark Street surface cars, an experience likened to Russian Roulette with a carbine.

David Condon
Chicago Tribune, *May 22, 1972*

Wrigley Field is almost the last of the old neighborhood ballparks, and the antiquity of the place [it was built in 1914, two years after Fenway Park opened in Boston] and the absence of night ball there [the Wrigley family believed that the crowds and the noise would be an affront to nearby residents] remind us what the game once felt like and how it fitted into the patterns of city life.

Roger Angell

pre-8/8/88

I'd play for half my salary if I could hit in this dump all the time.

Babe Ruth

It is a park, with spiders and grasshoppers and vines an inch around on the playing field. The vines come into bloom in mid-May. The morning glories open up pale blue and pink and purple and are shut again by noon. The greenish-white flowers of the bittersweet bloom inconspicuously against the ivy. There is Boston ivy with its eight-inch leaves that stick out from the brick a foot and a half and are clipped by the ground crew before every home stand. There is Baltic ivy with its shiny, leathery leaves that stay green all winter, and the high-climbing Virginia creeper, whose five-leaflet clusters turn reddish-orange in the fall. That is when the bunches of grapes hang purple on the grapevines and the bittersweet berries turn red, but in the spring there are flowers where the fruit will be.

E. M. Swift
on Wrigley Field

Wrigley Field is a classic midwestern cross between penurious efficiency and charm.

E. M. Swift

The ivy, many would say, is what puts the ubiquitous adjective in Beautiful Wrigley Field. . . . In the lineup of polyester ballparks, its loveliness is not only in its verdant complexion, but in the attitude it expresses, an appreciation of aesthetic virtue too often bygone in a sport of the heart.

Lonnie Wheeler

There's too much nature in that ballpark.

Harry Chiti
catcher (1950–52, 1955–56)

Wrigley Field was actually built in 1914 by a man named "Lucky Charlie" Weeghman. He owned the Chicago Whales of the short-lived Federal League, which lasted four seasons, 1912–1915. The park, then called Weeghman Park, was completed in time for the 1914 opener at a cost of $250,000, and it seated 14,000 fans. By December of 1918, William Wrigley Jr. had become the majority stockholder, Lucky Charlie had resigned, and Weeghman Park had become Cubs Park. It was renamed Wrigley Field in 1926 when construction was started on the upper deck.

E. M. Swift

The great joy in my life is to come out to Wrigley Field now. Coming out here is better than going to a psychiatrist. It's real therapy for me.

Ernie Banks

Wrigley Field was the first ballpark to install an organ, the first to have a Ladies Day.

E. M. Swift

Old men, playing dominoes across the hearth, like to say that Phil Wrigley was the last of the true baseball men because he is the only owner who still holds, in the simple faith of his ancestors, that baseball was meant to be played under God's own sunlight. I know better. Having blown the chance to be the first with lights, Mr. Wrigley just wasn't going to do it at all.

Bill Veeck Jr.

Wrigley Field was scheduled to debut lights in 1941 (the Cincinnati Reds had introduced them to the game in 1935). But then came Pearl Harbor, and the club sold its lights, already purchased, to the government for use in shipyards to aid the war effort.

Wrigley Field—hallowed ground for Cubs fans.

Wrigley Field is such an important part of people's lives. It really is, worldwide. . . . Went to the Vatican and had an audience with the pope in '69, and he's talking about Wrigley Field.

Ernie Banks

Wrigley Field is a Peter Pan of a ballpark. It has never grown up and it has never grown old. Let the world race on—they'll still be playing baseball in the friendly confines of Wrigley Field, outfielders will still leap up against the vines, and the Cubs—well, it's the season of hope. This could be the Cubbies' year.

E. M. Swift

The Okefenokee Swamp is quick compared to Wrigley Field's grass.

Don Sutton

Los Angeles Dodgers Hall of Fame pitcher (1966–80, 1988)/ broadcaster

That's why the Cubs like a lot of sinker-ballers out there; keep the ball on the ground.

Don Sutton
on the slow infield at Wrigley

Rafael Belliard couldn't play there; he'd get lost.

Don Sutton
on the height of the infield grass at Wrigley Field

Another of Wrigley Field's charms, the Andy Frain ushers, are generally accepted as the best in the business—polite, efficient and neat; men who will lead you to your seat and not accept a tip.

E. M. Swift

A fad. A passing fad.

Philip Wrigley
on night baseball, 1935

And on the seventh day the Lord rested, and came to beautiful Wrigley Field, to watch the Chicago Cubs play His own game, on His own green grass, under His own lights.

From the play "Bleacher Bums"

All along the street I noticed yellow signs put up in the lower windows of the little houses: "No Night Baseball"—a response to the rumor, back in midsummer, that the postseason games in Chicago might be played under some temporarily installed floodlights in order to placate the demands of the networks for night ball and its vast audiences and numbers.

Roger Angell
1984

I will take a pass on the lighting of Wrigley Field. . . . The loss of innocence is too precious to end up on a T-shirt. You do not strike commemorative coins for an execution.

Bernie Lincicome

Chicago Tribune, *August 8, 1988*

I learned the charm and the ambience and the great feel that Wrigley Field and day baseball gives the fans, but I recognized that if we were going to get into postseason play, it was going to be necessary [to have lights].

Dallas Green

general manager (1981–87)

Putting lights in Wrigley Field is like putting aluminum siding on the Sistine Chapel.

Roger Simon

sportswriter

Just like my dad remembered the Wrigley Field with the wooden fences, or my grandfather remembered the one with *no* fences, we have something to lock away in a secret part of our memory to be divulged at a later date to our children and grandchildren. From this day on, no baby born will know Wrigley totally without lights. . . . Times change. An era is over, a page has been turned.

Joe Mantegna
actor/Cubs fan

Mr. Wrigley told once how his dad designed the park and how the park has some thrills for the fans built into it. For instance, the left-field and right-field walls are designed so they jut back a few feet in the corners so that there are parts of left-center and right-center that aren't as deep as down the lines at Wrigley Field.

Cal Neeman
catcher (1957–60)

Time hallows a place, investing it with memories and creating for each visitor a personal relationship. Nothing can diminish an arena where the great Alexander once pitched; where Hornsby scorched his singular line drives; where Ruth stood and, according to legend, "called his shot"; where late one afternoon in the twilight Hartnett delivered the most resounding home run in the history of Chicago; where Ernie Banks played for 19 years; where Ryne Sandberg set the standard at second base.

Donald Honig

The scoreboard . . . still stands handsomely overlooking the bleachers; so high, haughty, and distant that it has never been struck by a batted ball.

Lonnie Wheeler

Wrigley Field is a living thing, adapting to its environment.

Bill Veeck Jr.

11

RIVALRIES

IF YOU DIDN'T HONESTLY and furiously hate the Giants, you weren't a real Cub.

Joc Tinker

shortstop (1902–12, 1916)

New York's Mutuals and the Chicago White Stockings played their first game on July 6, 1870, at New York's Union Grounds. The White Stockings' 13–4 defeat at the hands of the Mutes was reported in the Chicago papers as disgusting, embarrassing, and probably a harbinger of the end times. . . . The game set the tone for what was to come—year after year after year. A rivalry featuring both metropolitan and athletic titans had been born.

Warren N. Wilbert

So tightly knotted was the intense competition between the two over the years, that by the end of their era of domination, in 1940, they had split some 1,152 ball games almost evenly, New York leading by the thinnest of margins, 581 wins to Chicago's 571! During that time they won a total of 29 pennants, 15 for New York and 14 for Chicago.

Warren N. Wilbert

Anson's club won a close-run pennant race with the New York Giants by just two games in 1885. It was the first time that the league's Chicago and New York teams found themselves in hand-to-hand combat for the top spot, creating a rivalry that would peak in intensity two decades later, with distant echoes resounding again in 1969.

Donald Honig

The admirers of the Giants came on to witness the games in force, and so certain were they that their pets would win that they wagered their money on the result in the most reckless fashion. . . . There was not a man in the delegation that accompanied the Giants that did not lose, and lose heavily, on the games, which went a long ways toward illustrating the glorious uncertainties of baseball.

Cap Anson

on a critical four-game series between New York and Chicago that ultimately determined the 1885 pennant, won by Chicago

If this game goes to Chicago by any trick or argument, you can take it from me that if we lose the pennant thereby, I will never play professional baseball again.

Christy Mathewson

immortal New York Giants pitcher, before the October 8, 1908, playoff game against the Cubs, necessitated by the infamous "Merkle Boner" incident on September 23, a game that could have meant the pennant for New York. In that game, the Giants' Fred Merkle, a base runner on first, failed to step on second base after Al Bridwell's apparent game-winning hit. The Cubs won the playoff, 4–2

On July 19, 1927, John McGraw Day was celebrated at the Polo Grounds, honoring the New York manager during his 25th anniversary year with the Giants. The foe that day? The Cubs, who beat the Giants, 8–5, putting Chicago in first place by percentage points.

Warren N. Wilbert

Yes, sir, that was a World Series game.

Leo Durocher

*manager (1966–72),
on the Cubs' 1–0 win over Tom
Seaver and the New York Mets,
July 14, 1969, at Wrigley Field.
The teams began their smolder-
ing rivalry that midsummer, as
New York chased the front-
running Cubs*

Unlike Mets fans, we can cheer a loser without becoming losers.

Jim Langford

I think I'm going to have an ulcer before this season is over.

Ron Santo

on the 1969 National League pennant race, in which the Cubs' 9½–game lead on August 13 evaporated to two games over the New York Mets just two weeks later

I got my revenge. I beat the Mets in the seventh game of the 1973 World Series.

Ken Holtzman

the only member of the 1969 Cubs to go on to play in a World Series (Holtzman was with the Oakland Athletics in '73)

The Cub and Cardinal fans in left field [at Busch] got on rather amiably. It happened that the Grateful Dead were in town, and a large group from St. Louis—Dead fans who had met in the Busch Stadium bleachers—had come to see both them and the Cardinals. Some of the left-field Wrigley regulars were also Deadheads. In their trademark tie-dyed T-shirts, they were known as Gary Matthews fans, but their hearts beat to the Dead. It was a peculiar bond. "There's a unity of Deadheads," one of the St. Louisans said. "We may have different teams, but we all love the Dead. There's really a strong relationship between Deadheads and baseball."

Lonnie Wheeler

On a night in 1975 in St. Louis, a Cardinals hitter rocketed the ball back to Cubs reliever Darold Knowles. The ball hit Knowles in his supporter cup so loudly the noise was heard up in the pressbox. Knowles fell to the ground, then somehow recovered—via instinct or competitive spirit or whatever—to throw the man out at first base before crumpling to the ground again. "He's a real pro; he didn't think of himself and got his man at first," Jack Brickhouse intoned on WGN-TV.

George Castle
author

It's a Cubs-Cardinals game, and it's the biggest thing in the Midwest.

Mark McGwire
Cardinals first baseman (1997–2001) and former single-season home run king

The fans make that rivalry. When we take the field for batting practice in St. Louis, we're getting booed—and cheered. Same goes for the Cardinals in Chicago. You get that kind of electricity in the air, and the McGwire-Sosa duel added more of that in 1998.

Mark Grace

The real pressure-raisers were the verbal duels with fans of a team the Cubs never played except in exhibition games. Far more than the Cardinals, the White Sox and their backers put a burr under the average Cubs fan.

George Castle

12

THOSE
FABULOUS FANS

WRIGLEY FIELD FANS TAKE the same attitude toward ads on the scoreboard that
the Sierra Club would take toward taco
stands along the trails of the Grand
Tetons.

Lonnie Wheeler

The unshirted, violently partisan multitudes in the Wrigley Field bleachers sustain the closest fan-to-player attachment anywhere in baseball.

Roger Angell

The Bleacher Bums are a marauding troupe, a raucous group that has a president, identifiable garb [yellow hardhats], a head cheerleader [pitcher Dick Selma], and a secretary named Lou Blatz, who is 71 years old and who in 1916 pitched for the Chicago Whales of the Federal League on a diamond that would eventually become Wrigley Field.

Skip Myslenski
journalist, Chicago Tribune, *1979*

The last Cub pennant came in 1945, followed by an interminable dry spell, which attained such proportions that it transformed long-suffering Cub fans from frustrated to philosophical.

Donald Honig

There are more fans of the Cubs in the world than any other baseball team. The Chicago Cubs are truly America's team. The reason we love the Cubs is because the Cubs are survivors and so are we.

Tom Dreesen

Cub fans, they love you, win, lose, or draw. They had a Cavarretta fan club in '44, '45. They'd bring me cookies.

Phil Cavarretta

I've never seen fans like that. The worse we played, the more they came. For fans to come out to Wrigley is an event. I don't now if the Cubs deserve it or not, but they've got a gold mine. People want to spend a nice summer day out at Wrigley. I would.

Terry Francona
outfielder/first baseman (1986)

What I've never forgotten, and I never will, is that I played for the greatest people in Chicago. As long as I've played this game, they are the greatest people that ever lived. . . . You hit .220 but give 100 percent, and they love you. . . . I think the people made me better than what I was.

Hank Sauer
outfielder (1949–55),
1952 National League MVP

Eighty-five percent of the people in this country work. The other 15 percent come here and boo my players.

Lee Elia

I did say some things I really feel bad about. I think it's changed my personality. You'd be a damn fool not to think they're the greatest fans in the world. They've suffered through defeat and still love the players. But when I made my comments about the fans, I honest to God was directing them at those people who went after [Keith] Moreland and [Larry] Bowa. I didn't mean the Chicago people in general. That was something I often hoped they would understand, but that was unfortunate. . . . I'll always be the guy who said something about the Chicago fans, and that's something I'll have to live with.

Lee Elia

Elia's widely reported negative comment regarding Chicago fans followed two post-game altercations with Cubs rooters that involved Moreland and Bowa, both of whom jumped into the stands after being provoked following a tough home loss to the Los Angeles Dodgers in 1983.

[Philip] Wrigley had been a pioneer in insisting that the broadcast of Cub games be made available to as wide an audience as possible. He did this not necessarily for profit but because he believed baseball belonged to its fans, particularly those who were unable to get to the ballpark.

Donald Honig

In my naïveté, I had not understood the vested partnership that beer held in the bleachers. It was a firm of four: sun, people, beer, and ball game. The pecking order was interchangeable, depending on the crowd, the weather, and the score.

Lonnie Wheeler

Some people have said that the Cubs have become famous for losing. . . . It is fairer to say that the team has become famous because it is beloved, that the loyalty and enthusiasm of Cub fans have created a unique aura. Losing teams have been known to be abandoned by their followers. . . . Cub fans have kept it all in perspective.

Donald Honig

Chicago Cubs fans are the greatest fans in the world. They've got to be.

Herman Franks

I'll always remember best the first time I stepped out on the mound. They gave me a standing ovation, which is what they do to every new player. They welcome you right in. . . . Everyone is cheering real loud and pulling for you.

Bruce Sutter
closer (1976–80)

The loyalty went both ways. The best times of my career—my most fun and my best days—were with Chicago.

Hank Sauer

There's no place you can go in the United States, any city or team, where, if you lose, they still get the support the people give you here. The fans here are the best.

Ron Santo

If my colonel ordered me to take a hill, no matter what the cost in life and limb, I'd ask to bring five Cub fans along for the charge. From the very moment they're born, they know pain, suffering, danger, and misery.

Jack Brickhouse

I smoke, I drink, and I stay out late, because God has made me a promise. He will not allow me to die before the Cubs win the World Series. He has assured me that, whatever happens in my life, I will not pass away before the Cubs win it all. The day it happens, I'll have to decide whether I even want to live anymore anyhow.

Dennis J. Flavin
impeccable Cubs fan

There is no such thing as an ex-Cubs fan!

Jim Langford

13

THE
LOCKER ROOM

WE SHALL NO LONGER endure the criticism of the respectable people because of drunkenness in the Chicago nine.

Albert Goodwill Spalding

*Chicago White Stockings
president, 1886*

Carousing had become such a problem with some Cubs players that Spalding, following Chicago's championship series loss in 1886 to the American Association's St. Louis Browns, traded star catcher Mike "King" Kelly to the National League's Boston Beaneaters for the then-astronomical sum of $10,000. Soon after, pitcher Jim McCormick and center fielder George Gore were also gone.

I had four or five different gloves in my locker that first spring training. Center field, that was a whole different thing out there. I felt lost out there. That was a long way from home, playing short, second, then going into the outfield. I wound up making that team as the everyday third baseman in 1982.

Ryne Sandberg

on the Cubs' attempts at finding the right position for their eventual star second baseman his first season with the club

These are the saddest of possible words:
Tinker to Evers to Chance.
Trio of bear Cubs fleeter than birds,
Tinker to Evers to Chance.
Ruthlessly pricking our gonfalon bubble,
Making a Giant hit into a double—
Words that are weighty with nothing
* but trouble;*
Tinker to Evers to Chance.

Franklin P. Adams
journalist/writer/poet,
immortalizing the Cubs' early
1900s double-play combination

Banks to Baker to Addison Street.

Jack Brickhouse
on the Cubs' early to mid-'50s
double-play combo, mimicking
Franklin Adams's immortal
"Tinker to Evers to Chance."
Addison Street refers to infielder
Gene Baker's occasional wild
throws to first, which often went
into the stands

I can tell by the people walking home after a game whether they've won or lost. When the Cubs lose . . . they trample the flowers a bit.

James Flanagan
Wrigley Field neighborhood resident

I was in three World Series and I haven't won one yet.

Phil Cavarretta

If the Cubs get any decent pitching, they'll have a chance in their division. It's like they're jinxed or something. It's like that billy-goat thing, although I think that's a bunch of talk. You've got to have the personnel.

Andy Pafko

When I was with the Cubs, we had the best swearing ball club in the National League. Profanity. I'm not kidding you. We had Cavarretta, Don Hoak, and Dee Fondy. There was an old couple who had box seats right behind the dugout and they couldn't take it anymore. We ran them right out of the ballpark. Every other word. It was awful.

Eddie Miksis

Sunday ball had been played in Chicago for two years without objection, but a pressure group called the Sunday Observance League succeeded in having the entire team arrested in the third inning on June 23, 1895, for "aiding and abetting the forming of a noisy crowd on a Sunday." Club president James Hart posted bail, and the Colts [Cubs] finished the game, whipping Cleveland, 13–4.

**Art Ahrens and
Eddie Gold**

Winning isn't everything. It's pretty big as a player for the team, but for the fans and the families, they just had a great time coming to the games. I think that kind of rubbed off on me—this is a fun game. I think players sometimes forget that.

Ryne Sandberg

The history of the Chicago Cubs in the 1950s is the story of a team caught in a quagmire, of non-swimmers in deep water, of broken-boned men in a foot-race, of drivers with an empty tank. The best that the team could manage to produce in that decade was three fifth-place finishes.

Donald Honig

HACKED OFF

During their major league careers, Hack Wilson, Hack Miller, Stan Hack, and Warren Hacker all played for the Cubs.

Cap Anson, Mordecai Brown, and those doggerel-united triplets Tinker, Evers, and Chance are only visiting ghosts at Wrigley, but others have left real spike marks on the turf and cast real shadows on the ivied walls: Grover Cleveland Alexander, Hippo Vaughn, Hack Wilson, Rogers Hornsby, Billy Herman, Lon Warneke, Dizzy Dean, Bill Nicholson, Andy Pafko, Ernie Banks, Billy Williams, Ron Santo, Ferguson Jenkins, Ryne Sandberg, Andre Dawson, Mark Grace, Rick Sutcliffe, and on, up to the latter-day shareholders in baseball's most durable and continuous cavalcade—the "bear cubs fleeter than birds" who will play on and on, as long as the ball is round and the game weaves its spell.

Donald Honig

The last Cub to lead the league in steals was Stan Hack in 1939, with 17. The team record for stolen bases, 67, was set by Frank Chance during the Roosevelt presidency—Teddy's.

Lonnie Wheeler

When a pitcher named Jack Harper beaned Frank Chance once too often for his liking, Chance traded for him, cut his salary by two-thirds, refused to pitch him, and drove him into retirement at the age of 28.

Doug Myers

When I was cold, my reflexes weren't the same, as far as hitting goes. I always felt like the pitcher was ahead of me. I couldn't wait for May 1. Things seemed to always turn around then. To start the season year in and year out and to be struggling like that was always an uphill battle for me. I had to work through that almost every year. There were many sleepless nights in April thinking about those 0-for-4s.

Ryne Sandberg

My favorite umpire is a dead one.
Johnny Evers

14

CUBS
NATIONAL LEAGUE
CHAMPION ROSTERS

No one in major league baseball history can match the continuous lineage of the Chicago Cubs, who actually predate the birth of the National League In 1876. During that span of 129 years, it is estimated that more than 1,760 players have donned Cubbie Blue [or White Stocking white], with 365 of them adorning the rosters of Chicago's 16 National League pennant-winning teams.

1876

52–14

Albert Goodwill Spalding, *manager*

Bob Addy, *right field*
Fred Andrus, *outfield*
Cap Anson, *third base*
Ross Barnes, *second base*
Oscar Bielaski, *outfield*
John Glenn, *left field*
Paul Hines, *center field*
Cal McVey, *first base*
Johnny Peters, *shortstop*
Al Spalding, *pitcher*
Deacon White, *catcher*

Starting lineups in bold

1880

67–17

Adrian "Cap" Anson, *manager*

Cap Anson, *first base*
Tommy Beals, *outfield/second base*
Tom Burns, *shortstop*
Larry Corcoran, *outfield/shortstop*
Abner Dalrymple, *left field*
Silver Flint, *catcher*
Fred Goldsmith, *pitcher/outfield*
George Gore, *center field*
Charlie Guth, *pitcher*
Mike "King" Kelly, *right field*
Tom Poorman, *outfield/pitcher*
Joe Quest, *second base*
Ned Williamson, *third base*

1881

56–28

Adrian "Cap" Anson, *manager*

Cap Anson, *first base*
Tom Burns, *shortstop*
Larry Corcoran, *pitcher*
Abner Dalrymple, *left field*
Silver Flint, *catcher*
Fred Goldsmith, *pitcher*
George Gore, *center field*
Mike "King" Kelly, *right field*
Hugh Nicol, *outfield*
Andy Piercy, *second base/third base*
Joe Quest, *second base*
Ned Williamson, *third base*

1882

55–29

Adrian "Cap" Anson, *manager*

Cap Anson, *first base*
Tom Burns, *second base*
Larry Corcoran, *pitcher*
Abner Dalrymple, *left field*
Silver Flint, *catcher*
Fred Goldsmith, *pitcher*
George Gore, *center field*
Mike "King" Kelly, *shortstop*
Hugh Nicol, *right field*
Joe Quest, *second base*
Milt Scott, *first base*
Ned Williamson, *third base*

1885

87–25

World Series Co-Champions
(with American Association
St. Louis Browns, 3–3–1)

Adrian "Cap" Anson, *manager*

Cap Anson, *first base*
Tom Burns, *shortstop*
John Clarkson, *pitcher*
Larry Corcoran, *pitcher*
Abner Dalrymple, *left field*
Silver Flint, *catcher*
Ed Gastfield, *catcher*
George Gore, *center field*
Mike "King" Kelly, *right field*
Ted Kennedy, *pitcher*
Bill Krieg, *outfield*
Jim McCauley, *catcher/outfield*
Jim McCormick, *pitcher*
Fred Pfeffer, *second base*
Jimmy Ryan, *second base/outfield*
Billy Sunday, *outfield*
Sy Sutcliffe, *catcher*
Wash Williams, *pitcher/outfield*
Ned Williamson, *third base*

1886

90–34

Adrian "Cap" Anson, *manager*

Cap Anson, *first base*
Tom Burns, *third base*
John Clarkson, *pitcher*
Abner Dalrymple, *left field*
Silver Flint, *catcher*
Jocko Flynn, *pitcher/outfield*
George Gore, *center field*
Lew Hardie, *catcher*
Mike "King" Kelly, *utility*
Jim McCormick, *pitcher*
George Moolic, *catcher*
Fred Pfeffer, *second base*
Jimmy Ryan, *right field*
Billy Sunday, *outfield*
Ned Williamson, *shortstop*

1906
116–36
Frank Chance, *manager*

Fred Beebe, *pitcher*
Mordecai "Three-Finger" Brown, *pitcher*
Frank Chance, *first base*
Johnny Evers, *second base*
Doc Gessler, *outfield/first base*
Jack Harper, *pitcher*
Solly Hofman, *utility*
Johnny Kling, *catcher*
Carl Lundgren, *pitcher*
Pat Moran, *catcher*
Pete Noonan, *first base*
Orval Overall, *pitcher*
Jack Pfiester, *pitcher*
Ed Reulbach, *pitcher*
Wildfire Schulte, *right field*
Jimmy Sheckard, *left field*
Jimmy Slagle, *center field*
Bull Smith, *pinch hitter*
Harry Steinfeldt, *third base*
Jack Taylor, *pitcher*
Joe Tinker, *shortstop*
Tom Walsh, *catcher*
Bob Wicker, *pitcher*

1907

107–45
World Champions
(World Series victors over Detroit Tigers, 4–0–1)

Frank Chance, *manager*

Mordecai "Three-Finger" Brown, *pitcher*
Frank Chance, *first base*
Kid Durbin, *pitcher/outfield*
Johnny Evers, *second base*
Chick Fraser, *pitcher*
Jack Hardy, *catcher*
Solly Hofman, *utility*
Del Howard, *first base/outfield*
Mike Kahoe, *catcher/first base*
Johnny Kling, *catcher*
Carl Lundgren, *pitcher*
Pat Moran, *catcher*
Orval Overall, *pitcher*
Jack Pfiester, *pitcher*
Newt Randall, *outfield*
Ed Reulbach, *pitcher*
Wildfire Schulte, *right field*
Jimmy Sheckard, *left field*
Jimmy Slagle, *center field*
Harry Steinfeldt, *third base*
Bill Sweeney, *shortstop*
Jack Taylor, *pitcher*
Joe Tinker, *shortstop*
Heinie Zimmerman, *utility*

1908

99–55
World Champions
(World Series victors over Detroit Tigers, 4–1)

Frank Chance, *manager*

Mordecai "Three-Finger" Brown, *pitcher*
Vin Campbell, *pinch hitter*
Frank Chance, *first base*
Andy Coakley, *pitcher*
Kid Durbin, *outfield*
Johnny Evers, *second base*
Chick Fraser, *pitcher*
Jack Hayden, *outfield*
Solly Hofman, *utility*
Del Howard, *first base/outfield*
Johnny Kling, *catcher*
Rube Kroh, *pitcher*
Carl Lundgren, *pitcher*
Bill Mack, *pitcher*
Doc Marshall, *catcher/outfield*
Pat Moran, *catcher*
Orval Overall, *pitcher*
Jack Pfiester, *pitcher*
Ed Reulbach, *pitcher*
Wildfire Schulte, *right field*
Jimmy Sheckard, *left field*
Jimmy Slagle, *center field*
Carl Spongburg, *pitcher*
Harry Steinfeldt, *third base*
Joe Tinker, *shortstop*
Heinie Zimmerman, *utility*

1910

104–50

Frank Chance, *manager*

Jimmy Archer, *catcher/first base*
George Beaumont, *outfield*
Mordecai "Three-Finger" Brown, *pitcher*
Alex Carson, *pitcher*
Frank Chance, *first base*
King Cole, *pitcher*
Johnny Evers, *second base*
Bill Foxen, *pitcher*
Solly Hofman, *center field*
Johnny Kling, *catcher*
John Kane, *utility*
Rube Kroh, *pitcher*
Fred Luderus, *first base*
Harry McIntyre, *pitcher*
Doc Miller, *pinch hitter*
Tom Needham, *catcher*
Orval Overall, *pitcher*
Big Jeff Pfeffer, *pitcher*
Jack Pfiester, *pitcher*
Ed Reulbach, *pitcher*
Lew Richie, *pitcher*
Wildfire Schulte, *right field*
Jimmy Sheckard, *left field*
Harry Steinfeldt, *third base*
Joe Tinker, *shortstop*
Orlie Weaver, *pitcher*
Heinie Zimmerman, *utility*

1918

84–45

Fred Mitchell, *manager*

Vic Aldridge, *pitcher*
Grover Cleveland Alexander, *pitcher*
Turner Barber, *outfield*
Paul Carter, *pitcher*
Tommy Clarke, *catcher*
Tom Daly, *catcher*
Charlie Deal, *third base*
Phil Douglas, *pitcher*
Rowdy Elliott, *catcher*
Max Flack, *right field*
Claude Hendrix, *pitcher*
Charlie Hollocher, *shortstop*
Pete Kilduff, *second base*
Bill Killefer, *catcher*
Fred Lear, *pinch hitter*
Les Mann, *left field*
Speed Martin, *pitcher*
Bill McCabe, *second base/outfield*
Fred Merkle, *first base*
Buddy Napier, *pitcher*
Bob O'Farrell, *catcher*
Dode Paskert, *center field*
Charlie Pick, *second base/third base*
Lefty Tyler, *pitcher*
Hippo Vaughn, *pitcher*
Roy Walker, *pitcher*
Harry Weaver, pitcher
Chuck Wortman, *second base/shortstop*
Rollie Zeider, *second base*

1929

98–54

Joe McCarthy, *manager*

Tony Angley, *catcher*
Clyde Beck, *third base/shortstop*
Footsie Blair, *utility*
Sheriff Blake, *pitcher*
Guy Bush, *pitcher*
Hal Carlson, *pitcher*
Kiki Cuyler, *right field*
Mike Cvengros, *pitcher*
Woody English, *shortstop*
Mike Gonzalez, *catcher*
Earl Grace, *catcher*
Henry Grampp, *pitcher*
Charlie Grimm, *first base*
Gabby Hartnett, *catcher*
Cliff Heathcote, *outfield*
Trader Horne, *pitcher*
Rogers Hornsby, *second base*
Claude Jonnard, *pitcher*
Pat Malone, *pitcher*
Norm McMillan, *third base*
Johnny Moore, *outfield*
Art Nehf, *pitcher*
Bob Osborn, *pitcher*
Ken Penner, *pitcher*
Charlie Root, *pitcher*
Johnny Schulte, *catcher*
Riggs Stephenson, *left field*
Danny Taylor, *outfield*
Zack Taylor, *catcher*
Chick Tolson, *first base*
Hack Wilson, *center field*

1932

90–64

Rogers Hornsby, Charlie Grimm, *manager*

Ed Baecht, *pitcher*
Vince Barton, *outfield*
Guy Bush, *pitcher*
Kiki Cuyler, *right field*
Frank Demaree, *outfield*
Woody English, *third base*
Burleigh Grimes, *pitcher*
Charlie Grimm, *first base*
Marv Gudat, *outfield/first base*
Stan Hack, *third base*
Gabby Hartnett, *catcher*
Rollie Hemsley, *catcher*
Billy Herman, *second base*
LeRoy Herrmann, *pitcher*
Rogers Hornsby, *outfield/second base*
Billy Jurges, *shortstop*
Mark Koenig, *shortstop*
Pat Malone, *pitcher*
Jakie May, *pitcher*
Johnny Moore, *center field*
Bobo Newsom, *pitcher*
Lance Richbourg, *outfield*
Charlie Root, *pitcher*
Bob Smith, *pitcher*
Riggs Stephenson, *left field*
Danny Taylor, *outfield*
Harry Taylor, *first base*
Zack Taylor, *catcher*
Bud Tinning, *pitcher*
Lon Warneke, *pitcher*
Carroll Yerkes, *pitcher*

1935
100–54
Charlie Grimm, *manager*

Clay Bryant, *pitcher*
Tex Carleton, *pitcher*
Hugh Casey, *pitcher*
Phil Cavarretta, *first base*
Kiki Cuyler, *outfield*
Frank Demaree, *center field*
Woody English, *third base/shortstop*
Larry French, *pitcher*
Augie Galan, *left field*
Johnny Gill, *pinch hitter*
Charlie Grimm, *first base*
Stan Hack, *third base*
Gabby Hartnett, *catcher*
Roy Henshaw, *pitcher*
Billy Herman, *second base*
Roy Joiner, *pitcher*
Billy Jurges, *shortstop*
Chuck Klein, *right field*
Fabian Kowalik, *pitcher*
Bill Lee, *pitcher*
Freddie Lindstrom, *outfield/third base*
Ken O'Dea, *catcher*
Charlie Root, *pitcher*
Clyde Shoun, *pitcher*
Tuck Stainback, *outfield*
Walter Stephenson, *catcher*
Lon Warneke, *pitcher*

1938
89–63

Charlie Grimm, Gabby Hartnett, *manager*

Jim Asbell, *outfield*
Clay Bryant, *pitcher*
Tex Carleton, *pitcher*
Phil Cavarretta, *outfield/first base*
Ripper Collins, *first base*
Dizzy Dean, *pitcher*
Frank Demaree, *right field*
Al Epperly, *pitcher*
Larry French, *pitcher*
Augie Galan, *left field*
Bob Garbark, *catcher*
Stan Hack, *third base*
Gabby Hartnett, *catcher*
Billy Herman, *second base*
Kirby Higbe, *pitcher*
Billy Jurges, *shortstop*
Newt Kimball, *pitcher*
Tony Lazzeri, *utility*
Bill Lee, *pitcher*
Bob Logan, *pitcher*
Joe Marty, *outfield*
Bobby Mattick, *shortstop*
Steve Mesner, *shortstop*
Ken O'Dea, *catcher*
Vance Page, *pitcher*
Carl Reynolds, *center field*
Charlie Root, *pitcher*
Jack Russell, *pitcher*
Coaker Triplett, *outfield*

1945
98–56
Charlie Grimm, *manager*

Heinz Becker, *first base*
Cy Block, *second base/third base*
Hank Borowy, *pitcher*
Phil Cavarretta, *first base*
Bob Chipman, *pitcher*
Lloyd Christopher, *outfield*
Jorge Comellas, *pitcher*
Paul Derringer, *pitcher*
Paul Erickson, *pitcher*
Paul Gillespie, *catcher/outfield*
Ed Hanyzewski, *pitcher*
Stan Hack, *third base*
George Hennessey, *pitcher*
Roy Hughes, *utility*
Don Johnson, *second base*
Mickey Livingston, *catcher*
Peanuts Lowrey, *left field*
Lennie Merullo, *shortstop*
Johnny Moore, *pinch hitter*
Bill Nicholson, *right field*
John Ostrowski, *third base*
Reggie Otero, *first base*
Andy Pafko, *center field*
Claude Passeau, *pitcher*
Ray Prim, *pitcher*
Len Rice, *catcher*
Ed Sauer, *outfield*
Bill Schuster, *utility infielder*
Frank Secory, *outfield*
Walter Signer, *pitcher*
Ray Starr, *pitcher*
Mack Stewart, *pitcher*
Hy Vandenberg, *pitcher*
Lon Warneke, *pitcher*
Dewey Williams, *catcher*
Hank Wyse, *pitcher*

BIBLIOGRAPHY

Ahrens, Art and Eddie Gold. *The Cubs: The Complete Record of Chicago Cubs Baseball.* New York: Macmillan Publishing Company, 1986.

Astor, Gerald and the National Baseball Hall of Fame and Museum, Inc., National Baseball Library. *The Baseball Hall of Fame 50th Anniversary Book.* New York: Prentice Hall Press, 1988.

Brown, Warren. *The Chicago Cubs.* Carbondale, Ill.: Southern Illinois University Press, 2001.

Castle, George and Jim Rygelski. *The I-55 Series: Cubs vs. Cardinals.* Champaign, Ill.: Sports Publishing Inc., 1999.

Cava, Pete. *Tales from the Cubs Dugout.* Champaign, Ill.: Sports Publishing Inc., 2000.

Chicago Tribune Company and Chicago Cubs. *Sammy's Season.* Lincolnwood, Ill.: Contemporary Books, 1998.

Chieger, Bob. *The Cubbies: Quotations on the Chicago Cubs.* New York: Atheneum, 1987.

Fulk, David and Dan Riley, edit. *The Cubs Reader.* Boston: Houghton Mifflin Company, 1991.

Gifford, Barry. *The Neighborhood of Baseball: A Personal History of the Chicago Cubs.* New York: E.P. Dutton, 1981.

Golenbock, Peter. *Wrigleyville: A Magical History Tour of the Chicago Cubs.* New York: St. Martin's Press. 1996.

Honig, Donald. *The Chicago Cubs: An Illustrated History.* New York: Prentice Hall Press, 1991.

Langford, Jim. *Runs, Hits & Errors.* South Bend, Ind.: Diamond Communications, Inc., 1987.

Langford, Jim. *The Game Is Never Over: An Appreciative History of the Chicago Cubs, 1948–1980.* South Bend, Ind.: Icarus Press, 1980.

Logan, Bob. *More Tales from the Cubs Dugout.* Champaign, Ill.: Sports Publishing Inc., 2003.

Logan, Bob. *So You Think You're a Die-Hard Cub Fan.* Chicago: Contemporary Books, Inc., 1985.

Muskat, Carrie. *Banks to Sandberg to Grace.* Chicago: Contemporary Books, 2001.

Myers, Doug. *Essential Cubs: Chicago Cubs Facts, Feats, and Firsts—from the Batter's Box to the Bullpen to the Bleachers.* Lincolnwood, Ill.: Contemporary Books, 1999.

Names, Larry D. *Bury My Heart at Wrigley Field: The History of the Chicago Cubs.* Neshkoro, Wis.: Sportsbook Publishing Co., 1989.

Ross, Alan. *Echoes from the Ball Park*. Nashville, Tenn.: Walnut Grove Press, 1999.

Ross, Alan. "Ernie Banks: Mr. Cub." *1996 Baseball Handbook: Ernie Banks Commemorative Edition*. Nashville, Tenn.: Athlon Sports Communications, 1996: 1–3.

Sandberg, Ryne. Interview with Pete Van Wieren and Don Sutton. TBS, Chicago Cubs vs. Atlanta Braves, 10 April 2004.

Skipper, John C. Take Me Out to the Cubs Game. Jefferson, N.C.: McFarland & Company, Inc., Publishers, 2000.

Thorn, John et al. *Total Baseball: The Official Encyclopedia of Major League Baseball*, Fifth Edition. New York: Viking Penguin, 1997.

Wheeler, Lonnie. *Bleachers: A Summer in Wrigley Field*. Chicago: Contemporary Books, 1988.

Wilbert, Warren N. *A Cunning Kind of Play: The Cubs-Giants Rivalry, 1876–1932*. Jefferson, North Carolina: McFarland & Company, Inc., 2002.

INDEX

Index

Index

Index

Index

Printed in the USA
CPSIA information can be obtained
at www.ICGtesting.com
JSHW022220140824
68134JS00018B/1172

9 781581 824216